THE LOW-CARB GOURMET

RECIPES, TIPS AND INSPIRATION FOR THE LOW-CARB LIFESTYLE

KAREN BARNABY

Photographs by Maren Caruso

RODALE

This edition first published in 2005 by
Rodale International Ltd
7–10 Chandos Street
London W1G 9AD
www.rodalebooks.co.uk

Photographs by Maren Caruso
Book design by Joanna Williams and Briony Chappell

A CIP record for this book is available from the British Library
ISBN 1-4050-8793-5

Printed and bound in China using acid-free paper.

1 3 5 7 9 8 6 4 2

This edition distributed to the book trade by Pan Macmillan Ltd

Notice
This book is intended as a reference volume only, not as a medical manual. The information given here is designed to help you make informed decisions about your health. It is not intended as a substitute for any treatment that may have been prescribed by your doctor. If you suspect that you have a medical problem, we urge you to seek competent medical help.

Mention of specific companies, organizations or authorities in this book does not imply endorsement by the publisher, nor does mention of specific companies, organizations or authorities in the book imply that they endorse it. Internet addresses given in this book were accurate at the time it went to press.

RODALE
LIVE YOUR WHOLE LIFE™

We inspire and enable people to improve their lives and the world around them

TO MY MOTHER

No longer beside me, but always in my heart

ACKNOWLEDGMENTS

I would like to give thanks to all of the moderators and members of lowcarb.ca who generously gave me permission to use their creations, writings and inspiration in this book. Here you are, in alphabetical order:

To Colin, Donald, Doreen, Fern, Judi, Kristine, Lisa N., Lisa P., Michelle, Nat, Norma June, Ruth and Wa'il. It's hard to remember what life was like before lowcarb.ca.

To Drew, the general manager at the Fish House in Stanley Park for supporting the Low-Carb Dinner Series long enough to make them a success; Daishinpan International, the owners of the Fish House in Stanley Park for all their support; Jackie for maintaining the database and for her never-ending low-carb enthusiasm; sous chefs Wayne and Josh for their help with the low-carb dinners at the Fish House; Wanda for low carbing along with me and assisting me in teaching low-carb cooking classes; everyone who has worked at the Fish House since 1999 for tolerating my 'eat meat, not wheat!' ranting.

To my always supportive father, who knew that low carbing made sense even in the 1960s; my sister Jennifer for her wonderful shopping trips to clothe my new body and her husband, Jim, who approved of them; and my sister Patty and her daughter Nora for learning to live in the low-carb light.

To the Vancouver and Canadian media for making my low-carb journey public and in turn giving others the courage to follow the same path; Cindy Evetts, Dawn, Paul, and Connie McCalla, Maureen Goulet and Ro-Anne Johnston for knowing that low-carb cooking classes were a good idea and offering the venues to have them in.

To Steven, Adrian, Richard and Simone for being great friends with hearty appetites.

And a very special thanks goes to my dogs, Io and Tobias, who were a constant source of distraction and joy.

And to Susan Wels and my agent, Carole Bidnick – huge hugs, kisses and indebtedness, always.

CONTENTS

INTRODUCTION

ALTHOUGH MY LIFELONG PASSION FOR FOOD ultimately has led to a successful career as a chef, author and teacher, it was once my greatest handicap. I used to think it was a cruel trick of fate to be able to feed myself so well. I am surrounded by food all day – buckets of chocolate, great desserts, artisan bread, buttermilk mashed potatoes. Imagine being in a place where you can eat whatever you want at any time. Before I started eating low carb, I grazed all day on this stuff plus sweets and Coke, and ate meals on top of it! I never even gave a second thought to what I was feeding myself. Once I realized the effect my grazing was having on my health, I found that it was hard to keep my hand and head out of the food and change a habit and addiction of years. I wanted to change my eating habits more than anything else. More than eating chocolate, ice cream or a piece of bread. What I wanted most of all was to be healthy, happy and free. I was a prisoner of food and it was controlling every aspect of my life.

Early on, when the cravings were overwhelming, I would physically remove myself from the food. I've had wistful times when I realized that there would be certain foods that I could never eat again; I actually went through a period of mourning.

Now when I hear people talk about deprivation, I am puzzled. Not having a roof over your head is deprivation, or not having food or water. Not having a piece of cake is not deprivation – it's a mature choice, and I finally can make that choice.

When I was growing up, my family ate in a way I suppose was normal for the 1960s: three square meals a day, no junk food, fizzy drinks only as a treat, sitting down to meals together in the dining room regularly – and never in front of the TV – and dessert only on weekends. My maternal grandmother lived with us and cooked for us during the week and my mother took over on weekends. It was under their expert and affectionate guidance that I started cooking when I was about nine years old. I have especially fond memories of the grand flurry of baking for Christmas.

Unfortunately, when puberty hit, I sought solace in sugar, sneaking sweets at every possible opportunity and stashing them in my pockets, spending my allowance on fizzy drinks and chocolate bars. I was an overweight pre-teenager plagued by ear infections and allergies.

In 1972, Dr Atkins released his first edition of *Diet Revolution* and high-protein diets were all the rage. Without a clue about what I was doing – and without even reading the book – I set about restricting my carbohydrates. I'd eat one extremely thin piece of bread, one tiny spoonful of potato and a thin sliver of dessert. It worked! I lost about 13.5 kg (30 lb) that summer, just in time for the beginning of high school. I felt energized! I felt great! But it was a short-term diet for me. It never occurred to me that this way of eating could be a lifestyle choice.

I managed to maintain that weight loss into my twenties, passing through a few years of vegetarianism and macrobiotics. But then I discovered alcohol and Italian food. All that pasta, risotto, polenta and red wine put me back on the road to ruin.

I was about 30 when I finally put a stop to daily wine drinking. To my surprise, I lost no weight. What I didn't realize was that I had replaced my wine habit with a huge sugar habit. For ten years I got fatter and fatter until I weighed nearly 109 kg (17 st) at the age of 40.

So, I jumped on the low-fat bandwagon and ate lots of oats with skimmed milk and bowls of brown rice with tuna, vegetables and lemon juice. The bowls of complex carbohydrates left me banging my head against the wall with insane cravings for dessert, so I ate loads of chocolate sorbet and bananas before falling into bed. After ten months, I had lost only 4.5 kg (10 lb) and my mood had not improved either. Little did I realize that I was eating more carbohydrates than I ever had before.

Miraculously, the answer fell into my hands in the form of the book *Protein Power,* by Drs Michael Eades and Mary Dan Eades. The book offered me a diet plan I could live with for the rest of my life. It allowed me to eat many of my favourite things and to eat them until I felt satisfied. There have been many benefits along the way: I lost 32 kg (5 st) and improved my blood pressure and cholesterol levels.

Of course, I'm brimming with advice and opinions, but I'll just leave you with this: don't be in such a great hurry to make changes that you can't enjoy yourself on the journey. I'm not advising you to eat high-carb foods – far from it – but I am suggesting that you shouldn't become so rigid that you are paranoid about the food you eat. To me, not eating a tomato because it contains carbohydrates is a form of insanity. If you take that approach, the enjoyment of food will continue to elude you.

I can't remember a time when I felt saner, happier and healthier than I do now. And this book is filled with plenty of fantastic recipes that will help you feel the same way.

LIVING LOW-CARB

So what is a low-carb diet, and how does it work? The premise of the various published programmes is that by controlling or restricting your intake of carbohydrates, you will control the release of insulin. Controlling insulin is the key that helps your body burn fat instead of storing it and that helps control appetite and cravings.

There's a vast difference between low-fat, calorie-restricted diets and low-carbohydrate diets. The standard low-fat, low-calorie weight-loss diet basically starves the body, causing both fat and muscle to be burned for fuel. You do lose weight, but the loss of lean muscle tissue will reduce your metabolic rate, eventually slowing the fat-loss process. With a properly planned low-carb programme, your body will burn fat and will preserve the lean muscle. If you exercise, you'll add lean muscle while losing fat, which will increase your metabolic rate and increase the fat-burning effect. Another difference between low-fat and low-carb diets is that most low-carbohydrate plans allow you to eat when hungry and to eat as much as you need to ease your hunger.

WHAT ABOUT CAFFEINE, ALCOHOL AND WATER?

Some low-carb plans recommend avoiding caffeine because it may trigger the release of insulin, while other plans don't make a comment one way or the other. If caffeine-containing beverages and foods do not affect your weight loss, then you might decide to continue to enjoy them. Other people may find it best to avoid caffeine because it stalls their weight loss or they experience effects such as jitters, nervousness and insomnia. Caffeine is most commonly found in coffee, but it is also present in teas, chocolate, colas and some other soft drinks, as well as some pain-relieving tablets and cough remedies. Read the label carefully if you're not sure.

Alcohol is generally considered low carb when in the form of unsweetened distilled spirits or dry wine. Moderation is the rule. One problem with drinking is that a few drinks may impair your craving judgment, leading to eating indiscretions and high-carb bingeing. Be aware, and be prepared.

Drinking lots of water is especially important when low carbing to flush out the metabolic wastes and byproducts of all that fat burning. If you're not used to drinking water, you may experience thirst as hunger and will eat solid food rather than drink a glass of water.

It is generally recommended that you drink 1.9 litres (64 fl oz) of pure, plain water, plus an additional 240 ml (8 fl oz) for every 11.34 kg (25 lb) you want to lose – every single day.

There are many tricks to help you consume your required amount of water. In addition to filtering, you might try adding a slice of fresh lemon or lime. This adds extra flavour with only a trace of carbohydrate. Some people find that drinking water from a plain bottle or sports bottle helps. If you don't like ice cold water, try drinking it at room temperature. Conversely, add some ice if you prefer it really cold.

Vegetables are, of course, carbohydrates. However, most contain a good deal of fibre and as fibre is not absorbed and therefore has no impact on glucose or insulin levels, it is not included in the carbohydrate count. This is why it is good to choose high-fibre carbs, such as green vegetables. You'll be able to have a larger portion and still keep your 'effective' carb intake low.

The nutritional information at the end of each recipe in this book shows the amount of 'effective' carbohydrate (i.e. the amount of carbohydrate after the fibre has been subtracted), as well as the amount of protein, fat and calories per serving.

Generally, plain meats, poultry and fish contain no carbs. But watch out for hidden carbs in commercially processed meats. They can have carbs added that you may not suspect – sausages may contain breadcrumbs, milk ingredients and sugars; bacon, ham and other cured meats can contain sugar, corn syrup or dextrose; and many tinned fish products contain sugar or starchy sauces. Always read the label to be sure.

Other sources of carbs that often get overlooked are coffee, plus any cream and sweetener used. These can add up quickly if you drink a lot of coffee throughout the day. Coffee has 0.8 carb grams for a 180-ml (6-fl-oz) cup – that's a small cup. Avoid any processed low-fat food. It's almost always high in carbs. Salad dressings and condiments such as mustard can add up, too. Make sure you measure your portions accurately, even on things like vegetables. (If you are being truly vigilant, don't forget to count the carbs in those breath-freshening mints and in sugar-free gum.) Spices, herbs and flavouring extracts have carbs, although usually a small amount is used to season a whole recipe; be watchful of things like curry powders and pastes used in larger quantities. Cheese and cream are also often overlooked as a source of carbs.

FAT FACTS

All fats found in fresh whole foods are good, healthy and sometimes vital. It is therefore wise to include a full spectrum of fats in your diet, which will work hard to keep you healthy and young-looking. This, of course, is not the message we have been getting in the popular media, and because of this we have built up an unhealthy guilt complex and fear of fat.

Certain fats are indeed bad for us. Trans fatty acids have been linked to raising 'bad' cholesterol (LDL) and lowering 'good' cholesterol (HDL); they are also suspected of being behind that 'stubborn fat' that won't leave no matter what we do. They are the result of processing oils through hydrogenation. Although at present trans fats do not need to be stated on the ingredients lists on products you can spot their presence, as they are also called hydrogenated fats or partially hydrogenated fats or oils. Avoid anything that has any hydrogenated oil in it.

Rancid fat is the other bad fat – fat that has been mutated by oxygen, heat, moisture and light. This fat is full of free radicals and can contribute to all the health and ageing problems associated with them. At first you might think that it would be easy to avoid this one. Just reading the word 'rancid' tends to make our noses wrinkle in disgust; however, we have been conditioned to accept rancid fats. The reason that dollop of butter is salty is to help preserve it and to cover up the rancid taste. Yes, butter is good for us, but rancid butter is not. That flax (linseed) oil in the refrigerator is liquid gold to some, but if it is rancid, it is worse than useless. We have to retrain our noses and taste buds to discern fresh good fats from rancid bad ones. This is one reason for using unsalted rather than salted butter.

This retraining can be done by finding supermarkets that sell their stock quickly, store their products properly, and rotate their stock on the shelf so that no old products linger there. Also check the expiry dates on products to help you find the freshest product.

Remember that the best fats come from fresh whole foods, so try making your own butter from some fresh, pure whipping cream. Add a bit of salt to taste, if you prefer it salty, and memorize the taste to compare with commercially prepared butter. If that is a bit too much work, just find the freshest unsalted butter you can, and taste that. When dealing with vegetable oils, try grinding the seeds up and then smelling the fresh aroma. Again, if this is too much of a bother, just get a good smell of the oil when you first open the bottle and memorize that fresh scent. As soon as you notice that the smell is off, get rid of it.

BEGINNING THE LIFESTYLE CHANGE

A life without all the bread or pasta you've been used to eating may seem daunting at first. But low carbing is an almost hedonistic way to eat. As low-carb eating becomes a way of life and you start feeling great, you'll wonder how you ever ate the way you did before. An important thing to remember is that it's not all about losing weight. Low carbing is also about regaining health and, for some people, their sanity.

You may want to look at what's coming up on your social calendar before you start changing your eating habits. If there are many birthdays, weddings and other celebratory occasions, it may not be the best time to start. It's really important that you get a good few weeks of strict low carbing under your belt to know what it feels like. But if you like challenges and have great willpower, you may find that you can breeze through these events without any problem.

The first few weeks of low carbing can be an odd, confusing time. We've been so used to relying on carbohydrates to fill our plates and stomachs that it takes a while to switch that train of thought. It also takes our bodies a while to get comfortable with the process. We experience lethargy, headaches and other symptoms as our bodies switch to using fat – our own fat.

In the long run, indulging a few times a year will not cause harm, but take heed! I have sadly seen too many people go back to bad carb eating after indulging on holidays such as Christmas and simply continue to eat this way only to wonder what happened come the end of January. For some people – myself included – carbohydrate consumption is an addiction and one bite can set you off on a downward spiral. The key is in knowing yourself and your limits.

With your new low-carb way of life, you will have many opportunities to make small changes that will turn into daily habits. These habits will become part of your way of life and ensure you future success.

STOCKING YOUR LOW-CARB GOURMET KITCHEN

When it comes to the protein element of our diets, low-carbers are spoilt for choice, as poultry, meat, game, fish and seafood are unrestricted – in fact this is one of the reasons why many people enjoy a low-carb diet so much!

It goes without saying but when buying fresh meat and fish, go for the freshest, best quality you can afford and you'll be rewarded with superior flavour. At the meat counter look for cuts that you haven't tried before – pork tenderloin, for example, is great for stir-fries, as is lamb. Chicken is always a favourite and many people do eat a lot of it, however this isn't an excuse to buy budget packs. Good quality free-range or organic chicken has far more flavour. And don't forget cold meats. Deli counters in supermarkets have an increasingly diverse range of meats on offer. If you are lucky enough to live near an Italian deli try some of their distinct and delicious cold meats. One of my favourites is Genoa salami – a fantastic garlicky salami that is great with a bit of cheese. Try it in Antipasto Skewers (page 36).

Fish is a favourite of mine so it's great that more and more varieties of fish are becoming widely available. Find a reliable supplier who has a good turnover and look for the freshest fish available. Frozen fish is better than nothing but buying fresh fish that is in season is the best way to ensure a great flavour. Seafood scares many people, which is a pity because it is usually quick to prepare and has a delicious flavour and texture: try the steamed clams on page 96 and you'll see what I mean. Tinned fish and seafood is another good protein option for low-carbers, so don't dismiss it out of hand. Olive-oil packed tuna, sardines and mackerel are all tasty and great for a snack.

As well as buying the best in fresh produce I like to keep my kitchen stocked with some good-quality staple ingredients. Here are just some of my favourites.

Cheeses I particularly like the Italian cheeses Parmigiano-Reggiano, Grana Padano and Pecorino Romano, which are good for grating, and add a real punch to food. Mozzarella di bufala, made from buffalo milk, is creamy and subtle in the best of ways. I've occasionally – although I blush to tell – eaten a whole one as a lunch on the run.

Dried porcini mushrooms These delicious mushrooms need to be soaked in a scant amount of hot water before being used. The soaking liquid is incorporated into the dish you are making to provide more intense flavour.

Italian plum tomatoes (tinned) Great for sauces and stews. They're much better than the domestic variety of tinned tomatoes because of their taste and texture.

Miso Made from soya beans this paste comes light, dark and in between. Besides its most common use as soup, miso makes a great marinade for oily fish, such as mackerel and salmon, as well as for beef steaks, pork chops and duck breast.

Mustard Mustard is a great way to add oomph to salad dressings, sauces and marinades. There are Dijon and whole-grain mustards as well as flavoured ones like tarragon, horseradish, green peppercorn and garlic.

Nuts and seeds The store I frequent has an array of very fresh nuts and seeds: almonds (whole, sliced and ground), walnuts, pecans, hazelnuts, and sesame, sunflower and pumpkin seeds. Don't forget unsweetened coconut – it's a nut too!

Oils Now on to my favourite area, the olive oil selection! Varietals, flavoured oils and extra-virgin.

It's not always easy to find but one of the flavoured oils that I think is great in mayonnaise is lemon-flavoured olive oil – replace one-quarter of the oil in the recipe with an equal amount of lemon-flavoured oil. It's also wonderful drizzled on roasted chicken or added to salad dressings. Don't use these flavoured oils for cooking or their wonderful fragrance will be lost.

There will be an overwhelming variety of oils infused with herbs, garlic and chillies. These are great for adding the final touch to food, from soup to nuts!

Nut oils can add a delicious accent to salads and vegetables. The most common are walnut, hazelnut, pumpkin seed and almond. I've also used roasted peanut and avocado oil. These should be combined with a less robust oil and not used full strength or for salad dressings. They really shine as flavourings.

A NOTE ABOUT SWEETENERS

For the recipes in this book I have used Splenda, a relatively new granular sweetener. Unlike some sweeteners, it does not break down when heated – so do not substitute other sweeteners.

One of the things I enjoy with fresh berries is a few drops of nut oil and a few drops of aged balsamic vinegar. The next time you're cooking green beans, asparagus or broccoli, try drizzling them with nut oil and then sprinkling on finely chopped nuts that match the oil. A little Parmesan cheese doesn't hurt either!

Olives If you're an olive lover, you'll find a vast array to choose from, many of which are deliciously spiced or stuffed. I love the green olives stuffed with anchovy and the ones stuffed with almonds.

Peppers If you like roasted red peppers and don't want to go to the trouble of roasting and peeling them yourself, there are now a number of different brands available, packed in either liquid or olive oil. I'm partial to the oil-packed variety.

Pesto As well as the classic basil pesto, sun-dried tomato and olive pestos are now widely available. Jars of ready-made pesto are a great standby when you don't have time or the ingredients to make your own.

Pickles and artichokes If you like pickles, you'll find many unusual varieties on the shelves. Asparagus, beans, onions and mixed pickles are particularly good with cold meats. I was never a fan of tinned artichoke hearts until I found them packed in olive oil. Besides using them in salads or as a dip, you'll find they are great for pizza toppings or enclosed in a wrapping of prosciutto or salami.

Preserved lemons These are gradually finding their way into more and more supermarkets. Preserved lemons give an indescribable flavour to stews, casseroles and salads (see Roasted Red Pepper and Preserved Lemon Salad on page 59). To use, discard the pulp and chop the peel.

Salt and pepper I use sea salt and a good-quality peppercorn in my peppermill. Sea salt is much milder and less caustic than regular salt. It also contains trace minerals. I'm a bit of a salt hound and look for it wherever I travel.

Good supermarkets now carry a variety of sea salts and even a few flavoured salts. One of my favourites for sprinkling on cooked food is Maldon Salt, which has beautifully crunchy flakes.

KAREN'S TOP 10 REASONS FOR LIVING A LOW-CARB LIFE

1. Achieving permanent fat loss and looking radiantly fabulous

2. Feeling a great sense of accomplishment about what you have achieved

3. Gaining the ability to move freely and having consistent energy all day

4. Preventing heart disease and high-blood pressure

5. Eliminating mood swings

6. Living long enough to see your children and grandchildren into adulthood

7. Watching aches and pains, headaches, and sometimes even migraines, mysteriously disappear and skin clear up

8. Being able to shop in 'normal' shops for clothing and to do all the things that 'normal' size people do

9. Controlling or preventing diabetes and eliminating the symptoms of Polycystic Ovary Syndrome (PCOS)

10. Living each day to the fullest with newfound health.

Vinegars A great selection of vinegars is now available in most supermarkets. I like to keep several ages of balsamic vinegar around. The youngest I use in cooking, the middle-aged are for salads, and the oldest are respectfully used by the drop. Besides balsamic, there are sherry vinegars and vinegars made from wine varietals like Zinfandel and Cabernet Sauvignon, as well as plain red and white wine vinegar. Good-quality vinegar does make a difference. To make a dressing with lots of depth, try using a blend of different vinegars and oils.

WHAT'S FOR BREAKFAST?

ONE OF THE QUESTIONS I HEAR MOST OFTEN IS: 'What can I eat for breakfast? I'm sick of eggs and bacon!'

I would like to see the commandment that says, 'Thou shalt have eggs and pork products for breakfast!' You know, you can eat *anything* for breakfast, because it's just another meal. I would go a little crazy eating just bacon and eggs, too, so I don't. I like leftovers. *You* are allowed to eat anything you want for breakfast.

When you're pressed for time – or even when you're not – it's good to have a few breakfast tricks up your sleeve. Think outside of that breakfast box! Here are some ideas.

Tin of tuna or salmon with mayonnaise

Flax Porridge (page 25)

Ham wrapped around a slice of cheese

Hard-boiled eggs or egg salad

Fresh mixed berries with cream

Egg and Sausage Muffins (page 26)

Pizza Quiche with Garlic Sausage (page 115)

Leftovers, leftovers, leftovers . . .

ALMOND PUFF PANCAKES

Makes 8 pancakes

These are really good and have passed in my cooking classes with flying colours! I like them with melted butter, sweetener and cinnamon.

When cooking these pancakes, don't fiddle around with them before they are ready to turn or they will break! Give them about 3 minutes to brown the first side before you attempt to turn them.

2 large eggs, separated
60 ml (2 fl oz) whipping cream
1 tsp Splenda
Pinch of sea salt
50 g (1¾ oz) finely ground almonds
¼ tsp baking powder
1 tsp unsalted butter

In a large bowl, mix the egg yolks, cream, sweetener and salt until smooth. In a small bowl, whisk the ground almonds and baking powder together; whisk into the yolk mixture until smooth.

Place the egg whites in a medium bowl and beat with an electric mixer until soft peaks form. Stir one-quarter of the whites into the yolk mixture to loosen it up and then fold in the remaining whites.

Heat a large heavy frying pan over medium heat. Add the butter and, when it melts, wipe it out of the pan. Form pancakes using 60 ml (2 tablespoons) of the batter for each pancake. Cook for about 3 minutes, or until lightly browned, and then gently turn over and cook for 2 minutes on the other side.

Per pancake. Carbohydrates: 0.15 g; Protein: 2.9 g; Fat: 0.9 g; Calories/kJ: 84/352

UPSIDE-DOWN GOATS CHEESE SOUFFLÉ

Makes 2 servings

Here's a great way to use leftover whites if you make your own mayonnaise (you'll need the whites from 4 or 5 eggs). A cheese of your choice can be used instead of goats cheese. For best results, use a frying pan that's about 22.5 cm (9 in) in diameter.

120ml (4 fl oz) egg whites
Sea salt and freshly ground black pepper
45g (1½ oz) unsalted butter
30g (1 oz) thinly sliced mushrooms
½ medium tomato, thinly sliced
100g (3½ oz) crumbled fresh goats cheese

Preheat the oven to 200°C/400°F/gas 6.

Place the egg whites in a medium bowl and season with salt and pepper. Beat with an electric mixer until soft peaks form.

Melt the butter in a large ovenproof frying pan (preferably nonstick) over high heat. Add the mushrooms, season lightly with salt and pepper, and cook for about 5 minutes, or until the mushrooms become soft but not brown. Arrange the tomato slices over the mushrooms.

Quickly fold the cheese into the beaten egg whites and spread evenly over the mushroom mixture.

Transfer the pan to the oven and bake for 8 minutes, or until golden on top. Remove from the oven and run a heatproof rubber spatula around the sides to loosen. Flip over onto a plate and serve.

Per serving. Carbohydrates: 6.8 g; Protein: 18.8 g; Fat: 32.1 g; Calories/kJ: 387/1,620

OMEGA WAFFLES/PANCAKES

Makes 6 x 10-cm (4-in) square waffles or 12 x 5-cm (2-in) pancakes

Colin – my friend and creative-cooking co-conspirator – came up with this wonderful recipe. I like to add a teaspoon of pure maple extract to the batter and slather the waffles with plenty of butter. The soya milk makes them very light in texture. The soya milk I use has only 1.1 grams of carbohydrates per cup, which makes it excellent for low-carb cooking. If you do not possess a waffle maker, you can fry the batter to make pancakes.

40 g (1½ oz) ground flaxseed (linseed)
60 g (2 oz) walnut pieces
50 g (1¾ oz) finely ground almonds
2 tsp ground cinnamon
¼ tsp sea salt
4 tbsp Splenda
4 large eggs
240 ml (8 fl oz) unsweetened soya milk
1 tsp baking powder

In a blender or food processor, combine the ground flaxseed (linseed), walnuts, ground almonds, cinnamon, salt and sweetener. Blend until the walnuts are finely ground.

In a large bowl, whisk the eggs and 120 ml (4 fl oz) of the soya milk. Add the walnut mixture and combine well. Cover and refrigerate for at least 1 hour or up to overnight.

When you are ready to make the waffles, stir in the baking powder and the remaining soya milk; beat well.

Set your waffle maker to high and, following the manufacturer's directions, cook the waffles until light brown.

To make pancakes, lightly grease a heavy frying pan and, when really hot, drop heaped tablespoons of the batter on to the surface, keeping them well separated. Cook for 2–3 minutes until the underside is browned, then turn over with a fish slice and cook the other side. Cook the remaining batter in the same way.

Per waffle. Carbohydrates: 3.7 g; Protein: 8.5 g; Fat: 16.7 g; Calories/kJ: 207/867

JUST THE FLAX MUFFINS

Makes 6 muffins

Flax adds great flavour and an extra dose of fatty acids to muffins. For fruity flax muffins, you can add blueberries, cranberries, raspberries, strawberries or chopped rhubarb.

Note: *Whey protein isolate powder can be bought from good health food shops or from websites specializing in low-carb products.*

90 g (3 oz) ground flaxseed (linseed)
30 g (1 oz) whey protein isolate powder
2 tsp baking powder
2 tsp ground cinnamon
½ tsp sea salt
240 ml (8 fl oz) plain soya milk
2 large eggs
60 ml (2 fl oz) vegetable oil
4 tbsp Splenda
1 tsp pure maple or vanilla extract

Preheat the oven to 180°C/350°F/gas 4. Coat a 6-cup muffin tin with nonstick cooking spray.

In a medium bowl, whisk together the ground flaxseed (linseed), whey protein, baking powder, cinnamon and salt.

In a small bowl, whisk together the soya milk, eggs, oil, sweetener and extract. Add to the dry ingredients and mix well. Let the mixture stand for a minute or two and then divide it evenly among the prepared muffin cups.

Bake for 30–40 minutes, or until the muffins are nicely browned. Let stand in the pan for a minute or two before removing.

Per muffin. Carbohydrates: 3.1 g; Protein: 9.2 g; Fat: 7.4 g; Calories/kJ: 183/766

FLAX PORRIDGE

Makes 10 servings

This porridge sticks to your ribs and is a great way to start the day. Below is the basic dry mix, which you can store in a plastic bag and use as needed.

125 g (4½ oz) ground flaxseed (linseed)
90 g (3 oz) wheat bran
90 g (3 oz) textured vegetable protein (TVP) or natural soya mince
2 tbsp soya protein isolate powder (see page 151)
¾ tsp sea salt

In a large resealable plastic bag, combine the ground flaxseed (linseed), bran, TVP, soya protein and salt. Seal and shake until well mixed. Shake well before every use.

To make the porridge: Place 120 ml (4 fl oz) of the flaxseed mix in a cereal bowl and stir in 160 ml (5 fl oz) hot (not boiling) water. Cover and let stand for a minute or so. Sweeten to taste and add cream or yogurt as desired.

Per serving (without sweetener and cream or yogurt). Carbohydrates: 2.8 g; Protein: 1.8 g; Fat: 7.4 g; Calories/kJ: 147/615

FLAX FACTS

Flax is good food! Besides being chock-full of essential fatty acids, it also, um, helps regulate bowel function. Flaxseed (linseed) is made up of 41 per cent oil, and more than 70 per cent of that is polyunsaturated fat. One of its unique features is the high ratio of alpha-linolenic acid (an omega-3 fatty acid) to linoleic acid (an omega-6 fatty acid). These two polyunsaturated fatty acids are called essential because the body cannot manufacture them from any other substances.

Flaxseeds (linseeds) can be purchased at health food shops. You can grind them yourself in a canister-type coffee mill or spice grinder. The seeds are too small and hard to grind properly in a blender or food processor. Ready-ground, or milled, flaxseed (linseed) is available, but it's usually a bit more expensive and more difficult to find.

Air, light and heat will make flax go rancid quickly. Fresh flax should have a 'grassy' aroma. If it smells like linseed oil, it's gone off. Do not boil or microwave flaxseeds. Use hot water, not boiling. Temperatures over 82°C (180°F) destroy the essential fatty acids.

EGG AND SAUSAGE MUFFINS

Makes 12 muffins

These are great for a breakfast on the go. Use any type of sausage you enjoy – just make sure they're high-quality, as many inexpensive sausages contain breadcrumbs. You can also add sautéed mushrooms or onions to the mix.

These muffins can be frozen and reheated in the microwave.

Note: *Flexible baking trays have been on the market for a few years and are great for preparing low-carb muffins, mini quiches and more. They don't have to be buttered or oiled, and the food pops right out. They're also dishwasher-safe.*

455 g (1 lb) sausages
12 large eggs
120 ml (4 fl oz) whipping cream
120 ml (4 fl oz) water
¼ tsp sea salt
170 g (6 oz) grated Cheddar cheese

Preheat the oven to 180°C/350°F/gas 4. Coat a 12-cup muffin tin with nonstick cooking spray.

Remove the sausage meat from the casings and crumble the meat into a large frying pan. Cook over medium heat, stirring to break up the pieces, for 5 minutes, or until browned. Divide the meat evenly among the prepared muffin cups.

In a large bowl, whisk together the eggs, cream, water and salt. Pour over the sausage and top with the cheese.

Bake for 20–30 minutes, or until the eggs are cooked through. Cool slightly and remove from the tins.

Per muffin. Carbohydrates: 1 g; Protein: 15 g; Fat: 15 g; Calories/kJ: 256/1,072

ASPARAGUS AND BRIE FRITTATA

Makes 4 servings

This is a Low-Carb Breakfast cooking class favourite. Thanks to Kristine, a lowcarber.org moderator, for sharing it!

340 g (¾ lb) asparagus spears
60 ml (2 fl oz) extra-virgin olive oil
1 garlic clove, crushed
8 large eggs
¼ tsp sea salt
Freshly ground black pepper
115 g (4 oz) Brie, rind removed and cut into small cubes

Preheat the oven to 230°C/450°F/gas 8.

Trim the woody ends from the asparagus and discard. Cut the asparagus on the diagonal into 5-mm (¼-in) slices, leaving the tips whole.

Heat the oil in a large ovenproof frying pan (preferably nonstick) over medium heat. Add the asparagus and cook, stirring, until bright green and tender-crisp, about 3–4 minutes. Add the garlic and cook for 1 minute, or until it sizzles.

In a large bowl, whisk together the eggs, salt, and pepper to taste. Add to the pan and cook over low heat until the edges start to set. With a heatproof rubber spatula, lift all around the sides of the frittata while tilting the pan, to allow the uncooked egg to flow underneath. Let cook for 1–2 minutes, then repeat. Scatter the cheese over the top and poke the pieces into the eggs with the spatula.

Transfer the pan to the oven and bake for 7–10 minutes, or until the eggs are set.

Remove the pan from the oven and let stand for a few minutes. Run the spatula around the edges of the pan to loosen the frittata. Transfer to a plate or serve from the pan. Cut into wedges.

Per serving. Carbohydrates: 3.6 g; Protein: 20.3 g; Fat: 32.1 g; Calories/kJ: 389/1,628

NIBBLES
AND
DIPS

IT'S A GRACIOUS TOUCH TO HAVE a few appetizers set out before dinner when you are entertaining, and it's always good to have something 'snackable' in the fridge. You can make a lot of impromptu 'snappy appys' with just a few ingredients. Try roast beef rolled with cream cheese, blue cheese and asparagus; prosciutto wrapped around mascarpone, pine nuts and a sliver of melon; ham rolled with herbed cheese and some tasty pickle.

There are other good potential starters, snacks and appetizers dotted throughout this book. Pared-down versions of main-course salads are always good (see Salads and Dressings, page 50). Or try items like these.

Stuffed eggs

To-Frites (page 82)

Quick Prawns, Scampi-Style (page 93)

Turkey Fillet with Pesto and Smoked Mozzarella (page 109), served cold

MUSHROOM TAPENADE

Makes about 350 ml (12 fl oz)

This is more than just a great appetizer (serve it with sliced cucumbers, cheese or hard-boiled egg) – it's also a fantastic omelette filling, steak condiment or seasoning for sauces and salad dressings. The tapenade keeps, tightly covered in the refrigerator, for up to one week.

You can use different mushrooms, such as oyster, shiitake or portobello. Just make sure to remove the woody stems.

455 g (1 lb) fresh mushrooms
180–240 ml (6–8 fl oz) extra-virgin olive oil
2 tsp chopped fresh rosemary leaves
¼ tsp sea salt
2 garlic cloves, crushed
4 anchovy fillets
1 tbsp drained capers
Freshly ground black pepper

Preheat the oven to 220°C/425°F/gas 7.

In a large bowl, toss the mushrooms with 3 tablespoons of the oil. Sprinkle with the rosemary and ¼ teaspoon salt; toss to season evenly. Spread out in a baking pan large enough to hold the mushrooms in a single layer. Bake for 20 minutes, giving the mushrooms a stir after 10 minutes. Some of the mushrooms will look dried out – this is fine.

Let the mushrooms cool and then coarsely chop them. Transfer to a food processor along with the garlic, anchovies and capers. Process to a coarse purée. With the motor running, slowly add enough of the remaining oil – about 120–180 ml (4–6 fl oz) – to form a juicy paste. Season to taste with pepper and additional salt.

Per 1 tbsp. Carbohydrates: 0.6 g; Protein: 0.8 g; Fat: 6.9 g; Calories/kJ: 66/276

BUTTERY TUNA AND CAPER MOUSSE

Makes about 350 ml (12 fl oz)

This can be the centrepiece of an antipasto plate or a dinner on its own.

2 x 185-g (6½-oz) tins Italian tuna packed in olive oil
3 tbsp drained capers
115 g (4 oz) unsalted butter, at room temperature
2 tbsp coarsely chopped fresh basil

Drain the tuna, discarding the oil. Place in a food processor with the capers and butter. Process until smooth. Transfer to a bowl and stir in the basil.

Per 1 tbsp. Carbohydrates: 0.1 g; Protein: 4.3 g; Fat: 8.4 g; Calories/kJ: 93/389

WHAT TO DIP?

Here are some munching alternatives to crisps, breadsticks and pretzels:

Cooked or raw asparagus

Cooked green or yellow beans

Cooked or raw broccoli

Cauliflower florets

Cooked brussels sprouts

Cabbage leaves

Celery sticks

Cucumber sticks

Spring onions

Small romaine lettuce leaves

Mangetout

Red, green or yellow pepper strips

Red and daikon, or mooli, radishes

Sticks of salami or other cold meats

Cherry tomatoes

Turnip sticks

Wedges of hard-boiled egg

Strips of cooked chicken breast

PRAWNS WITH PEPPERY GARLIC VINAIGRETTE

Makes 10 servings

This dish can also be served as a main course. Choose some recipes from the Vegetables chapter for a complete meal.

120 ml (4 fl oz) extra-virgin olive oil
10 garlic cloves, thinly sliced
60 ml (2 fl oz) red wine vinegar
4 tbsp finely chopped fresh parsley
1 tsp freshly ground black pepper
½ tsp sea salt
1.3 kg (3 lb) large prawns, peeled and deveined

Heat the oil in a small frying pan over medium heat. Add the garlic and cook until it starts to turn golden, about 3 minutes. Remove from the heat and cool.

In a small bowl, whisk together the vinegar, parsley, pepper and ½ teaspoon salt. Slowly whisk in the oil mixture.

Bring a large pot of water to a boil and season liberally with salt. (It should taste like sea water.) Add the prawns and stir to separate them. Cook until the prawns are opaque at the thick end, about 3–4 minutes. Drain immediately and spread on a platter. Pour the vinaigrette over the prawns, toss lightly to coat, and serve.

Per serving. Carbohydrates: 2.2 g; Protein: 27.8 g; Fat: 13.2 g; Calories/kJ: 244/1,021

FIVE-SPICE SESAME WALNUTS

Makes 350 g (12 oz)

*These spicy walnuts are nice to serve as a nibble before a Chinese meal. They keep for
2 weeks at room temperature if tightly covered – and if you can resist them for that long.*

2 tbsp Splenda
½ tsp cayenne pepper
½ tsp sea salt
1½ tsp five-spice powder
1 large egg white
1 tsp pure caramel extract
300 g (10½ oz) raw walnut halves
75 g (2½ oz) sesame seeds

Preheat the oven to 180°C/350°F/gas 4. Line a baking sheet
with parchment paper.

In a small cup, combine the sweetener, cayenne, salt and
five-spice powder.

In a medium bowl, beat the egg white with a whisk until foamy but not stiff. Add the
caramel extract, walnuts and sesame seeds. Stir the mixture to coat with the egg white.
Add the spice mixture and stir until evenly blended.

Spread out in a single layer on the prepared baking sheet. Bake for 10 minutes.
Stir the nuts with a spoon and bake for 5–10 minutes longer, until lightly browned.
Cool completely.

Per 50 g (1¾ oz). Carbohydrates: 3.7 g; Protein: 6.6 g; Fat: 23.7 g; Calories/kJ: 243/1,017

WARM SPINACH DIP

Makes about 700 ml (25 fl oz)

This warm dip is much tastier than the cold variety. You can even use it in place of creamed spinach!

2 tbsp unsalted butter
1 small onion, finely chopped (about 60 g/2 oz)
6 garlic cloves, crushed
60 ml (2 fl oz) chicken stock
115 g (4 oz) cream cheese
285 g (10 oz) ready-to-use spinach
115 g (4 oz) freshly grated Parmesan cheese
½ tsp cayenne pepper, or to taste
Sea salt and freshly ground black pepper

Melt the butter in a large pan over medium heat. Add the onion and garlic and sauté for 5 minutes, or until the onion is soft but not browned. Whisk in the stock and cream cheese. Bring to the boil, whisking constantly. Cook, stirring frequently, until the mixture thickens, about 4–5 minutes.

Remove from the heat and add the spinach, cheese and cayenne. Stir until the spinach wilts. Season to taste with salt and pepper, and serve.

Per 2 tbsp. Carbohydrates: 0.9 g; Protein: 2.2 g; Fat: 3.6 g; Calories/kJ: 45/188

CAPONATA

Makes about 480 ml (16 fl oz)

This is one of my favourite aubergine dishes of all time, and I am sure you will find a myriad of uses for it, too – with meat and fish, on salads, with cheese, as an appetizer. It keeps for up to a week in a tightly closed container in the refrigerator.

1 x 455-g (1-lb) aubergine
60 ml (2 fl oz) extra-virgin olive oil
1 celery stick, cut into julienne strips, 5 cm x 5 mm (2 x ¼ in)
1 medium onion, cut into 1.2-cm (½-in) lengthwise wedges
350 ml (12 fl oz) passata (sieved tomatoes)
8 green olives, pitted
8 black olives, pitted
1 tbsp drained small capers
Sea salt and freshly ground black pepper
1 tsp balsamic vinegar
1½ tsp coarsely chopped fresh parsley
Handful of fresh basil leaves

Preheat the oven to 180°C/350°F/gas 4.

Prick the aubergine several times with a fork, place on a baking sheet and bake for 30–45 minutes, until completely soft. Remove from the oven and slit the aubergine open on one side. Place in a colander, slit side down, to drain and cool completely.

Meanwhile, heat the oil in a large saucepan over medium heat. Add the celery and onion and sauté for 5 minutes, or until translucent. Add the passata, olives and capers. Cook, stirring occasionally, for about 10 minutes, or until slightly thickened.

When the aubergine has cooled, peel off the skin. Chop the flesh crosswise into 5-cm (2-in) pieces and stir gently into the tomato mixture. Simmer for 10 minutes. Season to taste with salt and pepper. Add the vinegar, parsley and basil and remove from the heat.

Per 2 tbsp. Carbohydrates: 2.6 g; Protein: 0.7 g; Fat: 4 g; Calories/kJ: 53/222

ANTIPASTO SKEWERS

Makes 8 skewers

You can serve these with Aioli (page 139) as a dip. While good off the grill, these can also be served ungrilled and just chilled.

8 thin prosciutto slices
8 small pickled peppers, stems and seeds removed
16 Kalamata olives, pitted
16 cherry tomatoes
8 courgettes (zucchini), cut into 2.5-cm (1-in) cubes
8 small mushrooms, stems cut flush with the caps
8 salami cubes, about 2.5 cm (1 in)
60 ml (2 fl oz) extra-virgin olive oil
1 tbsp freshly squeezed lemon juice
1 tbsp balsamic vinegar
1 garlic clove, crushed
½ tsp dried oregano
¼ tsp sea salt
¼ tsp freshly ground black pepper

Soak 8 bamboo skewers in cold water for 15 minutes and drain.

Wrap a slice of prosciutto around each pepper. Thread each skewer with the ingredients in this order: 1 olive, 1 tomato, 1 courgette (zucchini) cube, 1 prosciutto-wrapped pepper, 1 mushroom, 1 salami cube, 1 olive and 1 tomato. Place the skewers in a shallow baking dish.

In a small bowl, mix the oil, lemon juice, vinegar, garlic, oregano, salt and black pepper. Pour over the skewers and turn them in the marinade to coat them all over.

Preheat the grill and grill the skewers until the vegetables are tender, about 4–5 minutes.

Per skewer. Carbohydrates: 3.4 g; Protein: 5.1 g; Fat: 9.5 g; Calories/kJ: 129/540

PRAWN AND NORI ROLLS

Makes 4 servings

Ahh…tastes like sushi! This should be made right before serving. You can add some avocado to this, too. If you use frozen prawns, thaw them and lightly squeeze them dry. Fresh or frozen, they should be small.

170 g (6 oz) small cooked prawns
1 tbsp mayonnaise
1 spring onion, thinly sliced
2 nori sheets
¼ cucumber, seeded and julienned
1 tbsp toasted sesame seeds

Make sure that the prawns are well drained. Place in a small bowl and mix in the mayonnaise and spring onion.

Lay 1 nori sheet on a flat surface. Place half of the prawn mixture 2.5 cm (1 in) from the edge nearest you. Lay half of the cucumber pieces evenly beside the prawns. Sprinkle with half of the sesame seeds. Roll up tightly to enclose the filling. Repeat with the remaining ingredients to make a second roll.

Let the rolls stand for a minute to soften. With a very sharp knife, cut each roll into 6 pieces.

Per serving. Carbohydrates: 0.4 g; Protein: 0.3 g; Fat: 5.7 g; Calories/kJ: 54/226

PARMESAN-STUFFED EGGS WITH TOASTED ALMONDS

Makes 8 halves

This dish would be great served with a platter of Italian cold meats.

4 hard-boiled large eggs, peeled
2 tbsp mayonnaise
60 ml (2 fl oz) extra-virgin olive oil
30 g (1 oz) freshly grated Parmesan cheese
2 tbsp finely chopped toasted almonds
Sea salt and freshly ground black pepper
8 toasted almonds (garnish)

Cut the eggs in half lengthwise and use a thin, sharp knife to take a tiny slice from the bottom of each half so it will sit firmly in place after stuffing. Scoop out the yolks with a small spoon and place in a small bowl. Set the whites on a platter.

Mash the yolks with a fork until smooth. Mash in the mayonnaise.

Stir in the oil, a drizzle at a time, until it is completely incorporated and the mixture is soft and fluffy. You may not need all the oil. Stir in the Parmesan and chopped almonds. Season to taste with salt and pepper.

Using a small spoon, stuff the whites with the yolk mixture. Top each half with an almond. Serve immediately or chill.

Per egg half. Carbohydrates: 0.7 g; Protein: 4.8 g; Fat: 14.5 g; Calories/kJ: 153/640

SOUPS

SOUPS ARE WHAT WE SHOULD TURN TO WHEN WE'RE PRESSED
FOR TIME. Hot soups fit the bill when it's cold outside or when we just need something warm and soothing. Chilled soups are great for hot-weather eating. Many of the
soups in this chapter are one-bowl meals and can be frozen so you'll always have a quick
meal on hand.

For best flavour, don't wait until vegetables are on their 'last legs' before using them.
As for what to make, let your vegetable drawer be your guide. You can cram a lot more
celery, for instance, into a soup than you can eat raw (and it's a sure way to finish that
whole bunch sitting in the crisper)!

Garnishes are a way of turning a good soup into a great soup. Fairly plain vegetable soups
can benefit from a spoonful of Basil Pesto (page 134). I think almost any soup is good with
a little diced avocado added to your bowl! And fresh herbs like basil, dill or mint stirred in
just before serving will give the zing of freshness.

Here are some soups that can be main meals all by themselves.

Kale Soup with Turkey Meatballs (page 46)

Winter Vegetable Soup (page 49)

Thai Prawn Soup (page 45)

Quick Korean-Style Beef and Spinach Soup (page 47)

CHILLED CUCUMBER AND AVOCADO SOUP

Makes 4 servings

Cold soups are great to have in the summer. They're all the better if they require no cooking – like this one.

1 cucumber, peeled, seeded and chopped
2 ripe Haas avocados, stoned, peeled and chopped
2 spring onions, chopped
2 tbsp freshly squeezed lime juice
240 ml (8 fl oz) soured cream
240 ml (8 fl oz) cold water
Sea salt and freshly ground black pepper
2 tbsp chopped fresh coriander leaves

In a blender or food processor, combine the cucumber, avocados, spring onions, lime juice, soured cream and water. Process until smooth. Season to taste with salt and pepper. If the soup is too thick for your liking, thin it with water. Stir in the coriander. Serve immediately or cover and let chill.

Per serving. Carbohydrates: 6.1 g; Protein: 4.1 g; Fat: 25.2 g; Calories/kJ: 270/1,130

CONSIDER THE AVOCADO

It's a natural in salads and chilled soups and as a garnish for hot soups and spicy dishes. The avocado can even star in desserts and protein shakes. Packed full of healthy mono-unsaturated fat, the avocado should be included in your diet. It's also a great contributor of potassium and beta-carotene. Avocados are the highest fruit source of lutein, a phyto-chemical that helps protect against cataracts and macular degeneration.

It's also the highest fruit source of Vitamin E, a powerful antioxidant known to slow the ageing process and help protect against heart disease.

CREAM OF BROCCOLI SOUP

Makes 8 servings

Other vegetables can replace the broccoli: asparagus, spinach, red peppers, tomatoes, or more cauliflower (for Cream of Cauliflower Soup). I once made this soup with red Swiss chard stalks, and it was delicious!

455 g (1 lb) cauliflower
685 g (1½ lb) broccoli
2 tbsp extra-virgin olive oil
2 garlic cloves, crushed
2.4 litres (4¼ pints) chicken stock
1 tsp sea salt
1 tbsp Dijon mustard
1 tsp dried tarragon or other herb
Freshly ground black pepper
Whipping cream (optional)

Trim the cauliflower and broccoli and chop coarsely. (Peel and use the cauliflower core and the broccoli stems. Save a few tiny broccoli florets for garnishing.)

Heat the oil in a large pan over medium heat. Add the garlic and sizzle until it smells fragrant. Add the cauliflower, broccoli, stock and salt. Bring to the boil. Reduce the heat and cook at a lively simmer for about 20 minutes, or until the vegetables are tender. Stir in the mustard and tarragon. Let cool slightly.

Working in batches, transfer to a blender and process until smooth. Return the mixture to the pan. (If you're using a fibrous vegetable like asparagus, you may want to press it through a sieve to make it smoother.) Add the reserved broccoli florets and season to taste with pepper and additional salt. Thin with stock or water if the soup is too thick. Stir in the cream (if using).

Per serving (without cream). Carbohydrates: 3.6 g; Protein: 8.2 g; Fat: 4.7 g; Calories/kJ: 100/419

THAI PRAWN SOUP

Makes 4 servings

There is a wealth of opportunity for good eating from Southeast Asia when you stop focusing on the rice and noodles. This soup is a good example, and it's fast and easy, too!

Lemongrass is easy for me to find, but I always keep frozen kaffir lime leaves and galingale root. You can also freeze lemongrass. You can find these ingredients in well-stocked supermarkets or speciality grocers.

1.4 litres (2½ pints) water
3 shallots, thinly sliced
2 lemongrass stalks, lightly pounded and cut into 2.5-cm (1-in) pieces
2 tbsp fish sauce
4 fresh or dried galingale root slices
340 g (12 oz) medium prawns, peeled with tails intact
230 g (8 oz) small mushrooms, halved
6 kaffir lime leaves
3 tbsp freshly squeezed lime juice
2 or 3 whole Thai chilli peppers
2 tbsp coarsely chopped coriander leaves
3 spring onions, thinly sliced

In a large saucepan, combine the water, shallots, lemongrass, fish sauce and galingale root. Bring to the boil over medium heat and cook for 3 minutes.

Add the prawns and mushrooms. Cook, stirring occasionally, until the prawns turn pink and are cooked all the way through, about 3–4 minutes. Add the lime leaves, lime juice and chillies. Cover and remove from the heat. Let sit for 1 minute. Ladle into bowls and sprinkle with the coriander and spring onion.

Per serving. Carbohydrates: 4.3 g; Protein: 18.3 g; Fat: 1.5 g; Calories/kJ: 109/456

KALE SOUP WITH TURKEY MEATBALLS

Makes 4 servings

I think kale makes delicious soup. The meatballs turn this soup into a meal.

1 tbsp extra-virgin olive oil
1 small onion, finely chopped (about 60 g/2 oz)
2 garlic cloves, crushed
1 tsp chopped fresh rosemary leaves or ½ tsp dried rosemary, crumbled
685 g (1½ lb) chopped kale
1.4 litres (2½ pints) chicken stock
455 g (1 lb) minced turkey
1 large egg
2 tbsp very finely chopped spring onion
1 tbsp finely chopped fresh parsley
30 g (1 oz) freshly grated Parmesan cheese
Sea salt and freshly ground black pepper
Lemon slices (optional)

Preheat the oven to 180°C/350°F/gas 4.

Heat the oil in a large pan over medium heat. Add the onion, garlic and rosemary and cook for 5 minutes, or until the onion is soft but not brown. Add the kale and stock. Bring to the boil. Reduce the heat, partially cover the pot, and simmer for about 6–8 minutes, or until the kale is tender but is not yet discoloured.

In a medium bowl, mix the turkey, egg, spring onion, parsley and cheese. Form into 2.5-cm (1-in) balls. Lightly oil a baking dish large enough to hold the meatballs in a single layer. Add the meatballs. Bake for 10 minutes.

Add the meatballs to the soup and simmer, partially covered, for 5 minutes. Season to taste with salt and pepper. Serve garnished with lemon slices (if using).

Per serving. Carbohydrates: 4.3 g; Protein: 34 g; Fat: 18.4 g; Calories/kJ; 346/1,448

QUICK KOREAN-STYLE BEEF AND SPINACH SOUP

Makes 4 servings

This filling soup is a great lunch-in-a-hurry dish.

1 tbsp toasted sesame oil
230 g (8 oz) lean minced beef
1 spring onion, finely chopped
1 garlic clove, crushed
1 tbsp soy sauce
720 ml (25 fl oz) water or chicken stock
230 g (8 oz) fresh spinach, washed and trimmed
2 large eggs, beaten
2 tsp toasted sesame seeds
Sea salt and freshly ground black pepper

Heat the oil in a large heavy pan over medium heat. Add the beef and brown it, breaking up the pieces with a wooden spoon. Add the spring onion, garlic and soy sauce and stir for 30 seconds. Add the water or stock, bring to the boil and add the spinach. Cover and simmer for 5 minutes.

In a small bowl, mix the eggs and sesame seeds with a fork. Season with salt and pepper. Slowly pour into the pan while swirling the soup with the wooden spoon. Continue to stir for a few minutes until the eggs float to the top and form tiny 'flakes'.

Per serving. Carbohydrates: 2.1 g; Protein: 19.1 g; Fat: 19.8 g; Calories/kJ: 274/1,147

WINTER VEGETABLE SOUP

Makes 8 servings

It's wonderful to have a hearty soup like this, especially in the winter. I like to cut the vegetables into small pieces to get the flavour of them all in each mouthful. This soup is especially delicious with a swirl of Basil Pesto (page 134).

By grating your own Parmesan or Grana Padano cheese, you will have the added bonus of the rinds. Save the rinds when you can grate no more cheese from them and freeze them. Add them to soups, stews and tomato sauces. They will provide a savoury flavour and aroma.

3 tbsp extra-virgin olive oil
2 small sticks celery, finely diced
1 small onion, finely diced
1 tbsp finely chopped fresh parsley
2 garlic cloves, crushed
1.9 litres (3⅓ pints) chicken stock or water
480 ml (16 fl oz) canned Italian plum tomatoes with juice, finely chopped
125 g (4½ oz) diced turnips
125 g (4½ oz) diced daikon or mooli radish
150 g (5½ oz) finely chopped green cabbage
150 g (5½ oz) finely chopped kale
2 large Parmesan or Grana Padano rinds
1 bay leaf
Sea salt and freshly ground black pepper
Freshly grated Parmesan cheese

Heat the oil in a very large pan over medium heat. Add the celery, onion, parsley and garlic and sauté until lightly browned. Add the stock or water and tomatoes. Bring to the boil.

Add the turnips, daikon or mooli, cabbage, kale, cheese rinds and bay leaf. Season lightly with salt. Simmer for 1 hour, or until the vegetables are very tender and the soup has thickened. (If it is too thick, add additional water or stock.) Season to taste with pepper and additional salt. Remove the bay leaf and cheese rinds. Serve with cheese sprinkled on top.

Per serving. Carbohydrates: 7.5 g; Protein: 1.8 g; Fat: 5.3 g; Calories/kJ: 88/368

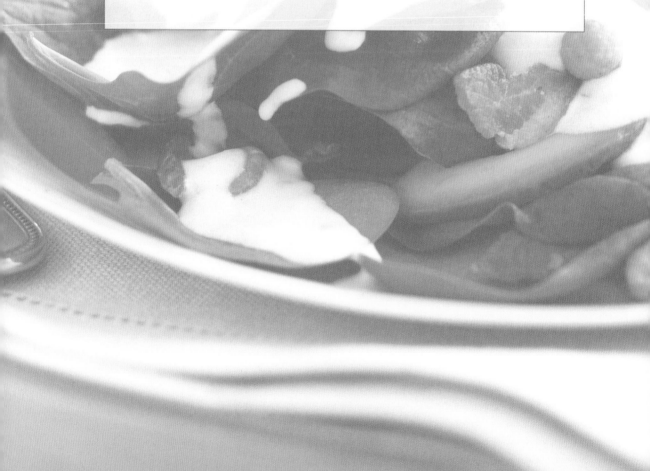

SALADS
AND
DRESSINGS

IF YOU TEND TO BUY THE SAME OLD ICEBERG LETTUCE or mixed leaves week after week, now is the time to get adventurous. Not that there is anything wrong with iceberg lettuce, especially a nice crisp wedge with a good blob of blue cheese dressing on it. There are different types of lettuce to discover – some great baby lettuce mixes, red leaf lettuce, romaine, endive, radicchio, chicory, watercress, rocket and mizuna.

No excuses – a quick tip is to wash and dry your lettuce all at once and store it in a resealable plastic bag lined with a paper towel, pressing the air out of it. You'll always have it ready when you want it.

There's no need to ever be bored with salads. These are the real workhorses of low-carb cuisine. Also, I'm a salad dressing snob. I don't buy bottled salad dressing and never have. I know that preparing dressings makes people nervous, but with the right recipe, you will have something more delicious and fresher-tasting than anything you could buy. If you're taking the time to make a wonderful, fresh salad, you should honour it by using a wonderful, fresh dressing.

Here are a few ideas to get you started.

Basic Vinaigrette (page 63)
Green Goddess Dressing (page 64)
Soured Cream and Spring Onion Dressing (page 64)
Japanese-Style Sesame Ginger Dressing (page 65)

PINE NUT AND PARSLEY SALAD

Makes 6 servings

This is the low-carb version of tabbouli, the wonderful Middle Eastern parsley salad. It's excellent with chicken. A traditional way of eating this is to wrap it up in a lettuce leaf.

You can mix the vegetables 4 to 6 hours in advance and add the dressing just before serving.

Note: *For variety, serve this salad minus the pine nuts and add a few chopped black olives, or add a sprinkling of feta cheese and diced avocado.*

SALAD

125 g (4½ oz) fresh parsley leaves, finely chopped
60 g (2 oz) fresh mint leaves, coarsely chopped
60 g (2 oz) seeded and finely chopped tomatoes
40 g (1¼ oz) seeded and finely diced cucumber
2 thinly sliced spring onions
75 g (2½ oz) pine nuts, coarsely chopped

DRESSING

2 tbsp freshly squeezed lemon juice
½ tsp finely chopped garlic
¼ tsp sea salt
5 tbsp extra-virgin olive oil
½ tsp ground allspice
¼ tsp ground cinnamon

To make the salad: In a large bowl, mix the parsley, mint, tomatoes, cucumber and spring onion. Sprinkle with the pine nuts. Cover and refrigerate until needed.

To make the dressing: Just before serving, combine the lemon juice, garlic and salt in a small bowl. Stir well. Slowly beat in the oil. Stir in the allspice and cinnamon. Pour over the parsley mixture and toss to coat.

Per serving. Carbohydrates: 3.6 g; Protein: 4.3 g; Fat: 18.3 g; Calories/kJ: 192/804

WARM CAULIFLOWER, BACON AND EGG SALAD WITH SPINACH

Makes 6 servings

This is a very succulent salad with great texture. I think it goes very well with white fish like halibut or cod. And leftovers are very good cold.

685 g (1½ lb) cauliflower, trimmed
6 hard-boiled large eggs, peeled
285 g (10 oz) ready-to-use spinach
8 bacon rashers, cut into 1.2-cm (½-in) pieces
2 finely chopped spring onions
120 ml (4 fl oz) extra-virgin olive oil
80 ml (3 fl oz) white wine vinegar
1 tbsp Dijon mustard
Sea salt and freshly ground black pepper

Cut the cauliflower evenly into 2.5-cm (1-in) pieces and set aside.

Cut the hard-boiled eggs into 6-mm (¼-in) slices. Place the spinach in a large bowl and add the eggs.

Fry the bacon in a medium frying pan over medium heat until crisp. Remove the bacon with a slotted spoon and add to the spinach. Add the spring onion, oil, vinegar and mustard to the pan and bring to a simmer, stirring constantly. Remove from the heat.

Bring a large pan of water to the boil and season liberally with salt. (It should taste like sea water.) Add the cauliflower and cook for about 6–7 minutes, or until it is tender but still has some texture. Drain immediately, tossing well to remove the water. Add the cauliflower to the spinach.

Bring the contents of the frying pan to the boil and pour over the salad. Toss gently. Season to taste with salt and pepper. Serve immediately.

Per serving. Carbohydrates: 4.6; Protein: 12.6 g; Fat: 28 g; Calories/kJ: 327/1,369

CUCUMBER SALAD WITH PEANUTS, COCONUT AND LIME

Makes 4 servings

This is one of my favourite salads. I think it's just delicious with prawns. Serve it with simple meat dishes or as part of a Thai or Indian feast. If you don't have the black mustard seeds, don't worry! But do try to use freshly roasted peanuts for best flavour.

2 tbsp dried unsweetened dessicated coconut
60 ml (2 fl oz) boiling water
300 g (10½ oz) cucumber cut into 5-mm (¼-in) cubes
75 g (2½ oz) unsalted roasted peanuts
2 small chilli peppers, finely chopped
2 tbsp freshly squeezed lime juice
½ tsp sea salt
1 tbsp vegetable oil
¼ tsp black mustard seeds

In a small bowl, combine the coconut and boiling water. Let stand until cool.

In a large bowl, combine the cucumber, peanuts and chillies. Add the coconut and mix well.

In a cup, mix the lime juice and salt. Just before serving, heat the oil over high heat in a small frying pan. Add the mustard seeds. When they pop, pour them into the lime mixture. Pour over the cucumber mixture and toss gently. Serve immediately.

Per serving. Carbohydrates: 5.2; Protein: 4.7 g; Fat: 13.6 g; Calories/kJ: 159/666

SPINACH SALAD WITH BACON, TOMATO AND AVOCADO

Makes 4 servings

You can make this salad even more scrumptious by adding chopped hard-boiled eggs and a few slivers of red onion. It goes well with a steak or simply cooked chicken.

285 g (10 oz) ready-to-use spinach
1 large ripe tomato, cut into thin wedges
1 ripe Haas avocado, stoned, peeled and cut into thin wedges
225 g (8 oz) bacon, cooked until crisp and then crumbled
2 tbsp unsalted roasted peanuts (optional)
Soured Cream and Spring Onion Dressing (page 64)

Place the spinach in a large bowl. Top with the tomato, avocado, bacon and peanuts (if using). Pour the dressing over the salad, toss well and serve.

Per serving. Carbohydrates: 4 g; Protein: 7.3 g; Fat: 32 g; Calories/kJ: 334/1,398

OVEN-FRIED BACON

If you like to eat bacon but don't like the messy splatters, you can cook a lot of bacon in advance with this oven method and simply reheat it as needed.

It's best to use a large dish that is not too deep, such as a rimmed baking sheet. You need to have enough surface area to brown the bacon and the baking sheet or tray must be deep enough to hold the fat. You may want to cover the sheet with foil for easy cleanup.

Position an oven rack in the middle of the oven and preheat the oven to 200°C/400°F/gas 6. Lay the bacon rashers in rows on the baking sheet. The pieces can touch but not overlap. Bake for 5–6 minutes, then rotate the sheet from front to back and continue baking for 5–6 minutes longer. If you use thick-cut bacon, increase the time.

Transfer the cooked rashers to paper towels to drain. When they're cool, you can lay the rashers between sheets of parchment paper, place in a covered container and refrigerate for up to 4 days, or freeze up to 6 months.

ROASTED RED PEPPER AND PRESERVED LEMON SALAD

Makes 4 servings

Serve this with grilled chicken or lamb, or 'meaty' fish – such as tuna or swordfish. Roasted peppers and preserved lemons can be found in the speciality aisles of good supermarkets or gourmet food shops.

6 tinned, jarred or freshly roasted and peeled red peppers
1 garlic clove, crushed
60 ml (2 fl oz) extra-virgin olive oil
¾ tsp ground cumin
¼ tsp smoked or regular paprika
¼ tsp freshly ground black pepper
1 preserved lemon, pulp removed and rind diced
Sea salt and freshly ground black pepper
30 g (1 oz) coarsely chopped fresh parsley

Coarsely chop the peppers and place in a large bowl. Stir in the garlic, oil, cumin, paprika, pepper and lemon rind. Season to taste with salt and pepper and toss in the parsley. Cover and refrigerate.

Per serving. Carbohydrates: 4.5 g; Protein: 1.3 g; Fat: 14.1 g; Calories/kJ: 152/636

TO STORE PARSLEY . . .

I think we've all faced limp or even rotten bunches of parsley hiding in the salad drawer of the refrigerator. Here's a great method for storing parsley. Pluck the parsley clusters from the stems – and I mean the little clusters of leaves from the little branched stems – then wash and dry thoroughly. Place in a large plastic container – a yogurt container works well for this – and punch several holes in the lid. The parsley will stay fresh and ready to use for at least 3 weeks.

WARM STEAK SALAD
WITH CREAMY SALSA DRESSING

Makes 2 servings

This is also delicious served with leftover roast beef or chicken instead of the steak.

340 g (12 oz) sirloin steak
Extra-virgin olive oil
Sea salt and freshly ground black pepper
230 g (8 oz) seeded and finely chopped ripe tomato
80 ml (3 fl oz) soured cream or crème fraîche
2 tbsp finely chopped coriander leaves,
1 tbsp freshly squeezed lime or lemon juice
1 jalapeño or other small hot chilli pepper, seeded and finely chopped
1 large romaine lettuce, chopped

Rub the steak on both sides with the oil and season with salt and pepper. Grill, barbecue or sear until done to your liking.

In a small bowl, mix the tomato, soured cream or crème fraîche, coriander, lime or lemon juice, jalapeño pepper to taste and ½ teaspoon salt.

Place the lettuce on a platter. Slice the steak and arrange it on the lettuce. Spoon the tomato mixture over the steak.

Per serving. Carbohydrates: 7 g; Protein: 42.8 g; Fat: 17.7 g; Calories/kJ: 374/1,566

SESAME, MANGETOUT AND WHITE RADISH SALAD

Makes 6 servings

Colourful and cool on the eyes, this goes well with roast pork and can be served alongside any Asian-style meal.

Sea salt
455 g (1 lb) mangetout, stringed and trimmed
340 g (12 oz) daikon or mooli radish, peeled and cut into
   thin matchstick strips
1 large red pepper, cored and cut into thin strips
2 tbsp freshly squeezed lemon juice
2 tsp grated fresh ginger
2 tbsp soy sauce
60 ml (2 fl oz) toasted sesame oil
Freshly ground black pepper
1 tbsp toasted sesame seeds

Bring a large pan of water to the boil and season liberally with salt. (It should taste like sea water.) Add the mangetout and cook only until they turn bright green. Drain immediately, cool under cold running water then drain again and pat dry.

Place the mangetout in a large bowl. Add the radish and red pepper. Cover and refrigerate for up to 6 hours.

In a small bowl, whisk together the lemon juice, ginger and soy sauce. Slowly whisk in the oil and season to taste with salt and pepper. When you are ready to serve the salad, pour over the vegetables and toss well. Sprinkle with the sesame seeds.

Per serving. Carbohydrates: 5.5 g; Protein: 3.5 g; Fat: 10.1 g; Calories/kJ: 136/569

BASIC VINAIGRETTE

Makes 180 ml (6 fl oz)

You can go wild with variations of a basic vinaigrette dressing recipe. Fresh or dried herbs, garlic, shallots or pesto will make your salads come alive. A few spoonfuls of soured cream turn it into a creamy dressing. You can make a Greek dressing by adding garlic and oregano. You can even add mashed raspberries or strawberries and a touch of sweetener to the basic vinaigrette.

You can also add dimensions of flavour with different vinegars and oils, singly or blending several into the vinaigrette. Use balsamic vinegar in place of the red wine vinegar. Or substitute walnut oil for half of the olive oil and you'll have vinaigrette that's great on asparagus or broccoli.

The most important element in the vinaigrette — or any salad dressing, for that matter — is salt. The dressing should taste slightly salty in the bowl. Remember, it has to cover a lot of water-filled vegetables. And in my humble opinion, a lot of vinaigrettes go a little too heavy on the vinegar.

2 tsp Dijon mustard
2 tbsp red wine vinegar
¼ tsp sea salt
120 ml (4 fl oz) extra-virgin olive oil
1 tsp freshly squeezed lemon juice
Freshly ground black pepper

In a small bowl, mix the mustard, vinegar and salt. Let stand until the salt dissolves.

While whisking or mixing with a hand-held blender, slowly pour the oil into the vinegar mixture. The dressing should thicken a bit and be evenly mixed. Add the lemon juice. Season with pepper and additional salt, if needed.

Per 1 tbsp. Carbohydrates: 0.3 g; Protein: 0 g; Fat: 9 g; Calories/kJ: 81/339

GREEN GODDESS DRESSING

Makes about 350 ml (12 fl oz)

This makes a great dip or a sauce for meat or vegetables, especially steak and asparagus.

120 ml (4 fl oz) mayonnaise
120 ml (4 fl oz) soured cream
30 g (1 oz) chopped spring onion tops
2 tbsp chopped fresh chives
2 tbsp chopped fresh parsley
2 tsp chopped fresh tarragon or 1 tbsp dried tarragon
3 anchovy fillets or 1 tbsp anchovy paste
1 tbsp freshly squeezed lemon juice
Sea salt and freshly ground black pepper

In a blender or food processor, combine the mayonnaise, soured cream, spring onion, chives, parsley, tarragon, anchovy and lemon juice. Process until smooth and light green. Season to taste with salt and pepper. Transfer to a bowl and refrigerate.

Per 1 tbsp. Carbohydrates: 0.4 g; Protein: 0.3 g; Fat: 4.7 g; Calories/kJ: 45/188

SOURED CREAM AND SPRING ONION DRESSING

Makes about 480 ml (16 fl oz)

Why buy when you can make a versatile dressing that tastes this good?
You can add a couple of cloves of crushed garlic to turn this into a creamy garlic dressing. Or add a few spoonfuls of Basil Pesto (page 134) for a creamy basil dressing. Alternatively, try some crumbled feta cheese and oregano for a creamy Greek dressing.

180 ml (6 fl oz) soured cream
120 ml (4 fl oz) mayonnaise
120 ml (4 fl oz) water
120 ml (4 fl oz) vegetable oil
2 tbsp white vinegar

2 tbsp finely chopped spring onion tops
2 tsp garlic powder
1 tsp Worcestershire sauce
¾ tsp sea salt
½ tsp dried basil
Hot-pepper sauce

In a small bowl, combine the soured cream, mayonnaise, water, oil, vinegar, spring onion, garlic powder, Worcestershire sauce, salt, basil and hot-pepper sauce to taste. Whisk until smooth. Cover and refrigerate.

Per 1 tbsp. Carbohydrates: 0.1 g; Protein: 0.3 g; Fat: 3.9 g; Calories/kJ: 38/159

JAPANESE-STYLE SESAME GINGER DRESSING

Makes 350 ml (12 fl oz)

This is excellent as a dip or dressing for meat, fish (especially salmon) and vegetables.
   Note: *This dressing will thicken as it sits. You can use water to thin it out.*

80 ml (3 fl oz) soy sauce
2½ tbsp tahini
1½ tsp toasted sesame oil
1 tbsp brown rice or white wine vinegar
1 tbsp finely grated fresh ginger
1 tbsp Splenda
60 ml (2 fl oz) water
80 ml (3 fl oz) vegetable oil
2 tbsp toasted sesame seeds

In a food processor or blender, combine the soy sauce, tahini, sesame oil, vinegar, ginger, sweetener and water. Blend until smooth. With the motor running, pour in the vegetable oil in a thin stream. Add the sesame seeds and pulse just enough to combine.

Per 1 tbsp. Carbohydrates: 0.5 g; Protein: 0.8 g; Fat: 4.9 g; Calories/kJ: 48/201

VEGETABLES

IT WAS A WISE PERSON INDEED WHO SAID, 'I didn't get fat from eating vegetables!'

One of the most fascinating and delicious aspects of low-carbing is taking the deep dive into the world of vegetables. A plainly cooked piece of chicken can be quite sexy when it's sitting beside a luscious vegetable dish such as Broccoli Italianissimo (page 69) or Spicy Roasted and Mashed Aubergine (page 74).

Vegetables don't always have to be crunchy. Many are delicious when cooked until soft, like Swede with Balsamic Vinegar and Browned Butter (page 71). Roasting is also a great way to bring a different character to familiar vegetables. And it's easy to add flair to vegetables with little effort: try fresh herbs, soured cream, toasted nuts and a matching nut oil.

Though not a vegetable, soya beans do grow on a plant and are another source of protein. So I've included a handful of tofu recipes, including Korean-Style Tofu (page 83) and To-Frites (page 82), to give you reason to experiment with it.

Here are a few of my favourites to get you started.

Green Beans with Eggs and Nutmeg (page 68)
Braised Fennel with White Wine and Parmesan (page 75)
Soy, Sake and Butter-Glazed Mushrooms (page 76)
Grilled Spinach with Four Cheeses (page 80)

GREEN BEANS WITH EGGS AND NUTMEG

Makes 6 servings

I really like the combination of nutmeg and vinegar that the Dutch use to season beans. This recipe takes it one step further. You can serve this at room temperature as well as warm, and it's great with salmon or other distinctively flavoured fish.

3 hard-boiled large eggs, peeled
1 tbsp coarsely chopped fresh parsley
1 tbsp finely chopped spring onion tops
⅛ tsp freshly grated nutmeg, or more to taste
Sea salt and freshly ground black pepper
455 g (1 lb) green beans, trimmed
3 tbsp extra-virgin olive oil
1 tbsp red wine vinegar

Grate the eggs into a bowl and toss with the parsley, spring onion and nutmeg. Season to taste with salt and pepper.

Bring a large pan of water to the boil and season liberally with salt. (It should taste like sea water.) Add the beans and cook until tender but still crisp, about 4–5 minutes. Drain the beans well and toss with the oil and vinegar. Add the egg mixture and toss well to coat the beans.

Per serving. Carbohydrates: 5.9 g; Protein: 4.1 g; Fat: 14.5 g; Calories/kJ: 189/791

BROCCOLI ITALIANISSIMO

Makes 4 servings

Delicious with anything remotely Italian. If you don't like anchovies, just leave them out.

455 g (1 lb) broccoli
3 tbsp extra-virgin olive oil
2 garlic cloves, crushed
2 anchovy fillets, finely chopped
Sea salt and freshly ground black pepper
30 g (1 oz) freshly grated Parmesan cheese

Cut the florets from the broccoli stems and trim the stalks. Cut the florets into bite-size pieces.

Bring a large pan of water to the boil and season liberally with salt. (It should taste like seawater.) Add the broccoli and cook until it's barely tender. Drain and cool under cold water; drain.

Heat the oil in a large frying pan over medium-high heat. Add the garlic and anchovies and sauté until the garlic starts to turn pale gold. Add the broccoli and season to taste. Stir and toss the broccoli until heated through. Sprinkle with the cheese.

Per serving. Carbohydrates: 3.1 g; Protein: 6.1 g; Fat: 12.2 g; Calories/kJ: 150/628

SCALLOPED SAVOY CABBAGE

Makes 6 servings

Scalloped vegetables are great when the weather turns cold. This cabbage goes well with all meats, but especially with pork, ham and sausages. Add a sprinkling of cheese, if you like, for the last 30 minutes of baking. To turn this into a meal, place sausages that you have browned on top of the cabbage for the last 30 minutes of cooking.

455 g (1 lb) Savoy cabbage
1 thinly sliced onion
60 g (2 oz) freshly grated Parmesan cheese
600 ml (1 pint) whipping cream
¾ tsp sea salt
Freshly ground black pepper

Preheat the oven to 180°C/350°F/gas 4. Cover a rimmed baking sheet with foil.

Remove the outer leaves of the cabbage and cut the head into quarters. Core and slice thinly. Place in a large bowl and toss with the onion and cheese. Transfer to a 32.5- × 22.5-cm (13- × 9-in) baking dish.

In a medium saucepan, bring the cream, salt and pepper to taste to the boil. Pour over the cabbage and cover tightly with foil. Place on the prepared baking sheet.

Bake for 45 minutes. Remove the foil and bake for 30 minutes longer. Let the cabbage stand for 10 minutes before serving.

Per serving. Carbohydrates: 6.2 g; Protein: 6.4 g; Fat: 38.8 g; Calories/kJ: 398/1,666

SWEDE WITH BALSAMIC VINEGAR AND BROWNED BUTTER

Makes 8 servings

In this recipe the balsamic vinegar balances the sweetness of the vegetable. Cut the swede into quarters with a large heavy knife before peeling. This makes them easier to handle.

You can make the swede purée up to 2 days ahead, cover and refrigerate. Bring to room temperature and reheat, covered, in a 200°C/400°F/gas 6 oven for 20–30 minutes.

I serve this for Christmas dinner, which is why the recipe makes a large amount.

1.8 kg (4 lb) swedes, peeled and cut into 2.5-cm (1-in) cubes
115g (4oz) unsalted butter
2 tbsp soured cream
Sea salt and freshly ground black pepper
2 tbsp balsamic vinegar

Place the swede in a large pan and cover with cold water. Bring to the boil and cook at a moderate boil until the pieces are tender, 45 minutes to 1 hour. Drain well.

Mash by hand or purée in a food processor. Return to the pan and stir in half the butter, the soured cream, and salt and pepper to taste. Stir over low heat until hot. Transfer the purée to a large gratin or baking dish.

Melt the remaining butter in a small saucepan over low heat until it turns a nut brown. Add the vinegar. Drizzle over the purée and serve immediately.

Per serving. Carbohydrates: 7.8 g; Protein: 1.8 g; Fat: 13.1 g; Calories/kJ: 161/674

BASIC CAULIFLOWER MASH

Makes 6 servings

The great thing about mashed-cauliflower dishes is that they can be reheated beautifully.

To make a purée that's very thick, purée the cauliflower alone. Spoon it into a cheese-cloth-lined sieve, place over a bowl to catch the drips, cover and refrigerate overnight. Then reheat gently and add the remaining ingredients.

You can season Cauliflower Mash with roasted garlic, Basil Pesto (page 134), fresh garlic, chopped sun-dried tomatoes, wasabi paste and Dijon mustard.

900 g (2 lb) cauliflower, trimmed
Sea salt
60 ml (2 fl oz) whipping cream
60 g (2 oz) unsalted butter
30 g (1 oz) freshly grated Parmesan cheese
60 g (2 oz) cream cheese

Cut the cauliflower, including the core, into 2.5-cm (1-in) pieces. Bring a large pan of water to the boil and salt lightly. Add the cauliflower and cook over medium heat until completely tender, 20–30 minutes.

Drain the cauliflower in a colander. With a bowl or small plate, press on the cauliflower to remove all the water. Toss the cauliflower and continue pressing out the water. This step is very important to the texture of the dish.

Transfer the cauliflower to a food processor. Add the cream and purée until completely smooth. If you like a chunkier texture, mash by hand, adding the cream after the cauliflower is mashed. Return to the pan.

When you are ready to serve the purée, heat over low heat, stirring constantly. Add the butter, Parmesan and cream cheese. Stir until incorporated. Season to taste with salt, if necessary. Serve immediately.

Per serving. Carbohydrates: 4.6 g; Protein: 5.4 g; Fat: 16.6 g; Calories/kJ: 193/808

BASIC CAULIFLOWER 'RICE'

Makes 6 servings

This goes with almost anything saucy. My sous chef and good friend Wayne just loves it with crumbled feta, olive oil and chopped tomato on top. The variations are endless: a bit of curry powder, some grated lemon rind to go with fish, or some chilli powder.

900 g (2 lb) cauliflower, trimmed
60 g (2 oz) unsalted butter
2 garlic cloves, crushed
1 tsp sea salt
2 spring onions, thinly sliced
Freshly ground black pepper

Grate the cauliflower, including the core, using the medium holes of a grater or the grater attachment of a food processor. With your hands, squeeze out as much water as you can. (This may not be necessary for some cauliflower as they vary in degree of wetness.)

Melt the butter in a large heavy frying pan over medium heat. Add the garlic and sauté until the garlic sizzles. Add the cauliflower, sprinkle with the salt, and stir-fry until tender-crisp, about 5–8 minutes. The length of time will depend on the cauliflower.

Stir in the spring onions and season to taste with pepper. Check the seasoning and serve.

VARIATION

For a Pan-Asian taste, use oil instead of butter. Scramble 2 eggs in the oil after sautéeing the garlic. Add chopped, cooked meat or prawns, give a few stirs, then add the cauliflower. Serve with soy sauce at table.

Per serving. Carbohydrates: 4.3 g; Protein: 3.1 g; Fat: 8.4 g; Calories/kJ: 109/456

SPICY ROASTED AND MASHED AUBERGINE

Makes 6 servings

Lovers of Indian food will recognize this as bharta. This dish is great served warm or cold as a dip.

2 medium aubergines, about 900 g (2 lb) total, cut in half lengthwise
90 ml (3 fl oz) vegetable oil
1 small onion, finely chopped
2 tbsp finely chopped fresh ginger
1 tbsp crushed garlic
2 tsp ground cumin
1 tsp sweet paprika
1 tsp ground coriander
½ tsp cayenne pepper
230 g (8 oz) tomatoes, coarsely chopped
2 tbsp chopped fresh coriander
Sea salt and freshly ground black pepper

Preheat the oven to 180°C/350°F/gas 4.

Oil a pan large enough to hold the aubergine halves in a single layer. Place the halves, cut side down, in the pan. Roast until the flesh is soft, about 1 hour. Cool slightly. Scoop the pulp from the aubergine skin into a sieve and let drain while you prepare the rest of the ingredients.

Heat the oil in a large heavy frying pan over medium-high heat. Add the onion and sauté until golden brown. Add the ginger, garlic, cumin, paprika, ground coriander and cayenne. Stir for a minute longer. Add the tomatoes and cook over high heat, stirring frequently, until the tomatoes thicken and become pulpy.

Mash in the aubergine, reduce the heat, and stir until slightly thickened. Remove from the heat and stir in the coriander. Season to taste with salt and pepper.

Per serving. Carbohydrates: 8.5 g; Protein: 2.4 g; Fat: 12.7 g; Calories/kJ: 168/703

BRAISED FENNEL WITH WHITE WINE AND PARMESAN

Makes 6 servings

Fennel is tasty served raw and crunchy in salads or softly braised as in this recipe. It goes well with chicken, pork or fish.

Fennel is usually sold with most of the long fronds removed, but occasionally you get to see the bulbs in their full glory.

2 × 455 g (1 lb) fennel bulbs
60 g (2 oz) unsalted butter
Sea salt and freshly ground black pepper
120 ml (4 fl oz) dry white wine or chicken stock
60 g (2 oz) freshly grated Parmesan cheese

Preheat the oven to 160°C/325°F/gas 3.

Trim the base and stems from the fennel and cut each bulb into 6 wedges.

In a frying pan large enough to hold the fennel comfortably, melt the butter over medium heat. Add the fennel and season to taste with salt and pepper. Add the wine or stock and bring to a simmer.

Cover, lower the heat and let the fennel cook for about 15 minutes. Turn the wedges over, cover and cook until the liquid has evaporated and the fennel starts to turn golden. Turn over and colour the other side. Sprinkle with the cheese and serve. (You can also pop the pan under the grill to brown the cheese if you like.)

Per serving. Carbohydrates: 6.7 g; Protein: 4.6 g; Fat: 11.8 g; Calories/kJ: 175/733

SOY, SAKE AND BUTTER-GLAZED MUSHROOMS

Makes 4 small servings

A wonderful accompaniment to Asian meals, these mushrooms are also good as an appetizer or thinly sliced and tossed with a salad.

455 g (1 lb) extra-large white mushrooms
240 ml (8 fl oz) water
60 ml (2 fl oz) soy sauce
120 ml (4 fl oz) sake
2 tsp Splenda
4 fresh ginger slices, 1.2-cm (½-in) thick
2 tbsp unsalted butter
1 tsp toasted sesame seeds

Trim the mushroom stems flush with the caps and save the stems for another use.

In a large pan, combine the water, soy sauce, sake, sweetener and ginger. Bring to the boil and add the mushrooms. Cook at a medium boil, turning the mushrooms over every 5 minutes, for about 20 minutes, or until the liquid turns into a light glaze. Remove the ginger. Stir in the butter and sesame seeds.

Per serving. Carbohydrates: 8 g; Protein: 4.2 g; Fat: 7 g; Calories/kJ: 144/603

BASIC SPAGHETTI SQUASH

Makes 10 servings

My grandmother would stuff spaghetti squash with cooked minced beef and bake it until the squash was tender. She only did this occasionally, so it was a treat.

With the way it turns into tender but crisp shreds, spaghetti squash makes an interesting medium for different flavours. While I don't miss pasta – and I used to eat it almost every day – I do miss some of the flavour combinations. Spaghetti squash, as well as cauliflower, fits the bill as the vehicle.

After you cook the squash, you can divide the pasta-like shreds into small portions and freeze them.

Note: *To microwave the squash, place the cut and seeded halves in a microwaveable dish and add 1 cm (½ in) of water. Cover tightly with plastic wrap and microwave on high power for 10 minutes. The squash is done when the skin yields to firm pressure. Uncover and let cool before scraping out the shreds with a spoon.*

1 x 1.4-kg (3-lb) spaghetti squash

Preheat the oven to 180°C/350°F/gas 4.

With a sharp, sturdy knife, trim the stem end from the squash and split the squash in half lengthwise. Scoop out the seeds with a spoon. Lay each half, cut side down, in a large baking dish and add 1 cm (½ in) water to the pan. Cover tightly with foil and bake for 40 minutes. Remove from the oven, uncover and let cool.

With a spoon, scrape out the spaghetti-like shreds.

Per serving. Carbohydrates: 5.2 g; Protein: 0.6 g; Fat: 0.6 g; Calories/kJ: 29/121

SPAGHETTI SQUASH ARRABBIATA

Makes 8 servings

Spaghetti squash is a mild flavoured vegetable that gets along with all types of seasonings. I don't think of it as a substitute for pasta but as a wonderful vegetable in its own right. Try flavouring it with butter and nutmeg, Parmesan, chilli powder, coconut milk and curry powder. This recipe does make a lot of servings, but the leftovers freeze just fine.

2 tbsp extra-virgin olive oil
2 garlic cloves, crushed
60 g (2 oz) prosciutto, finely diced
1–2 hot chilli peppers, finely chopped
230 g (8 oz) tinned Italian plum tomatoes with juice, puréed
Sea salt and freshly ground black pepper
½ recipe Basic Spaghetti Squash (page 77)
60 g (2 oz) freshly grated Parmesan cheese

Heat the oil in a large pan over medium heat. Add the garlic, prosciutto and chillies to taste. Cook until the garlic turns golden.

Add the tomatoes. Turn the heat to low and cook until the mixture thickens slightly, about 20 minutes. Season to taste with salt and pepper.

Add the spaghetti squash and simmer until heated through, about 5 minutes. Stir in the cheese and serve.

Per serving. Carbohydrates: 6.2 g; Protein: 4.8 g; Fat: 6.3 g; Calories/kJ: 102/427

GRILLED SPINACH WITH FOUR CHEESES

Makes 6 servings

This is quick, easy and delicious. You can change the cheeses depending on your mood.

60 g (2 oz) grated Gruyère cheese
115 g (4 oz) ricotta cheese
60 g (2 oz) crumbled Gorgonzola or blue cheese
2 tbsp freshly grated Parmesan cheese
2 tbsp chopped fresh dill
1 large egg yolk
2 tbsp unsalted butter
1 garlic clove, crushed
570 g (1¼ lb) ready-to-use spinach
Sea salt and freshly ground black pepper

Preheat the grill. Lightly butter a 27.5- × 17.5-cm (11- × 7-in) baking dish.

In a large bowl, mix the Gruyère, ricotta, Gorgonzola or blue cheese, Parmesan, dill and egg yolk.

Melt the butter in a large pan over medium-high heat. Add the garlic and stir for a minute until fragrant. Pour into the baking dish. Add the spinach to the pan and sauté until wilted. Transfer to a strainer; drain well. Add to the baking dish and toss to coat with the butter. Season to taste with salt and pepper.

Evenly spread the spinach in the dish and dot the cheese mixture over the top. Grill about 15 cm (6 in) from the heat until cheese is golden on top and the spinach is heated thoroughly.

Per serving. Carbohydrates: 2 g; Protein: 10.5 g; Fat: 8.2 g; Calories/kJ: 177/741

COURGETTE, SOURED CREAM AND CHEESE BAKE

Makes 4 servings

You can use a fairly mild Cheddar for this dish, though if you prefer a cheese that packs more punch, use a mature Cheddar.

60 g (2 oz) unsalted butter
60 g (2 oz) finely chopped spring onion
1 garlic clove, crushed
455 g (1 lb) courgette (zucchini), trimmed and sliced 3-mm (⅛-in) thick
115 g (4 oz) grated Cheddar cheese
1 large egg
120 ml (4 fl oz) soured cream
½ tsp sea salt
2 tbsp chopped fresh basil or 1 tsp dried

Preheat the oven to 180°C/350°F/gas 4. Butter a 20- × 20-cm (8- × 8-in) baking dish.

Melt 1 tablespoon of the butter in a large frying pan over medium heat. Add the onion and garlic and sauté until the onion is translucent. Scrape into a large bowl.

In the same frying pan, melt the remaining butter over medium-high heat. Add the courgette (zucchini) and cook, stirring frequently, until all the moisture has evaporated and the courgette (zucchini) is tender. Transfer to a food processor and pulse until smooth.

Add the cheese, egg, soured cream, salt and basil. Pulse to combine. Add the onions and pulse once. Pour into the prepared baking dish.

Bake for 30 minutes, or until lightly golden.

Per serving. Carbohydrates: 4.7 g; Protein: 11.3 g; Fat: 28.7 g; Calories/kJ: 320/1,340

TO-FRITES

Makes 3 servings

Serve these with a good-quality ketchup or Aioli (page 139), for a great snack.

340 g (12 oz) firm tofu, drained
1 large egg
1 tbsp mayonnaise
1 tbsp Dijon mustard
¼ tsp sea salt
½ tsp paprika
½ tsp garlic powder
Freshly ground black pepper
115 g (4 oz) freshly grated Parmesan cheese
Sea salt

Preheat the oven to 200°C/400°F/gas 6. Line a baking sheet with parchment paper.

Cut the tofu into long, thin French fry-like sticks.

In a large shallow dish, beat the egg, mayonnaise, mustard, salt, paprika, garlic powder, and pepper to taste until well-combined. Spread the cheese out on a plate.

Add a few tofu sticks at a time to the egg mixture and roll them gently to coat on all sides. Transfer the tofu to the cheese plate and roll to coat on all sides. Transfer to the baking sheet.

Bake for 20 minutes. Pop under the grill for a minute or so to brown the tops. Sprinkle with the salt and serve. These are best served hot.

Per serving. Carbohydrates: 4.5 g; Protein: 36 g; Fat: 26.9 g; Calories/kJ: 400/1,674

KOREAN-STYLE TOFU

Makes 2 servings

This delicious dish makes a good introduction for people who think they don't like tofu. Try it for breakfast!

340 g (12 oz) medium-firm tofu, drained
2 tbsp soy sauce
1½ tsp toasted sesame oil
2 tbsp thinly sliced spring onion
1½ tsp toasted sesame seeds
1½ tsp dried chilli flakes, or to taste
2 large eggs
¼ tsp sea salt
1 tbsp vegetable oil

Slice the tofu into 6 pieces and lay out on several layers of paper towels to drain.

In a small bowl, mix the soy sauce, sesame oil, spring onion, sesame seeds and chilli flakes.

In a shallow bowl, beat the eggs and salt together using a fork.

Heat the vegetable oil in a large frying pan (preferably nonstick) over medium heat. Dip the tofu slices into the egg and place in the pan. Pour the remaining egg mixture over the tofu. Fry until golden brown on one side. Flip over and cook until golden brown on the other side. Transfer to a plate and drizzle with the soy sauce mixture.

Per serving. Carbohydrates: 4 g; Protein: 26.1 g; Fat: 27.3 g; Calories/kJ: 363/1,520

USING YOUR NOODLE

Lasagne needn't be a distant memory. Using the Pizza Quiche with Garlic Sausage (page 115) as the basis for 'noodles' was the brainchild of Lisa, a long-term low-carber. Absolutely brilliant!

LASAGNE 'NOODLES'
Makes 8 servings

The recipe makes 2 large egg sheets. You may think that isn't enough for a lasagne, but believe me, it is.

The egg sheets can be made a day in advance. You can use your favourite lasagne fillings with them. Alternatively, try them in Spinach, Ricotta and Pesto Lasagne (opposite) or Bolognese Lasagne (page 120).

230 g (8 oz) cream cheese, at room temperature
12 large eggs
240 ml (8 fl oz) whipping cream
½ tsp sea salt
Freshly ground black pepper
115 g (4 oz) grated full-fat mozzarella cheese
115 g (4 oz) grated mature Cheddar cheese

Preheat the oven to 180°C/350°F/gas 4. Generously butter two 32.5- × 22.5-cm (13- × 9-in) nonstick baking sheets. (If you don't have nonstick baking sheets, line yours with parchment paper and then butter the paper.)

Place the cream cheese in a food processor and pulse until smooth. Beat in the eggs, one at a time. Add the cream and salt and pepper to taste. Divide the mixture evenly between the prepared baking sheets. Sprinkle evenly with the mozzarella and Cheddar.

Bake for 20 minutes, or until set. Remove from the oven. Invert each egg sheet onto a separate baking sheet. Let cool on wire racks. Cover and refrigerate.

Per serving. Carbohydrates: 3.3 g; Protein: 17.7 g; Fat: 36 g; Calories/kJ: 408/1,708

SPINACH, RICOTTA AND PESTO LASAGNE

Makes 8 servings

If you can get really good ricotta, usually sold sealed in a plastic basket, I think it makes a huge difference. It's creamier than ricotta sold in a carton.

Homemade pesto and tomato sauce are best, but if you don't have them, use store bought.

570 g (1¼ lb) ready-to-use spinach
680 g (1½ lb) ricotta cheese
2 large eggs
⅛ tsp freshly grated nutmeg
½ tsp sea salt
60 g (2 oz) freshly grated Parmesan cheese
120 ml (4 fl oz) Basil Pesto (page 134)
360 ml (12 fl oz) Simple Tomato Sauce (page 134)
Lasagne 'Noodles' (opposite)
170 g (6 oz) grated full-fat mozzarella cheese

Preheat the oven to 180°C/350°F/gas 4.

Place the spinach and a scant amount of water in a large pan. Cover and cook over medium-high heat until wilted. Cool, squeeze out the water and chop finely.

Place the spinach in a large bowl. Stir in the ricotta, eggs, nutmeg, salt, Parmesan and pesto. Cover and refrigerate for up to 1 day.

Spread one-quarter of the tomato sauce in a 32.5- × 22.5-cm (13- × 9-in) baking dish. Carefully transfer 1 lasagne noodle to the dish. Spread with another quarter of the tomato sauce. Evenly spread the spinach filling on top.

Add more tomato sauce, the remaining lasagne noodle and the rest of the tomato sauce.

Bake for 35 minutes. Sprinkle with the mozzarella and bake for 10 minutes longer. Remove from the oven and let rest for 10 minutes before serving.

Per serving. Carbohydrates: 14.5 g; Protein: 43.3 g; Fat: 66.6 g; Calories/kJ: 836/3,499

FISH
AND
SEAFOOD

ONE OF MY FAVOURITE FOODS TO WORK WITH IS FISH. Fish cooking makes a lot of people nervous, and rightly so. Fish is usually one of the more expensive proteins, and no one wants to mess it up. My one huge piece of advice when cooking fish is this: it's better to undercook it than overcook it. And remember that any food will continue cooking once you take it off the heat. It's better to return it to the heat to cook more than have a dry and chewy piece of fish on your plate.

Fatty fish like salmon and mackerel are rich in omega-3 fatty acids, and all fish are an excellent choice for low-carbers. If you've never tried them, swordfish and tuna are wonderfully meaty fish. Fresh tuna will be a revelation as it in no way resembles tinned tuna.

I always look forward to the halibut season. While many fish are just fine frozen, I think that halibut loses its wonderful delicate texture after freezing. Cod, when it's treated gently and not overcooked to a state where it resembles cotton, can be as wonderful as halibut.

Clams and mussels are quick to prepare, and their stock is always delicious. In these recipes, clams and mussels can be used interchangeably.

These recipes will impress you fish lovers on any occasion.

Baked Halibut with Lemon Basil Vinaigrette (page 88)
Sole with Horseradish Cream Sauce (page 90)
Pancetta-Wrapped Salmon with Red Wine Butter (page 91)
Seared Tuna with Soy Wasabi Glaze (page 94)

BAKED HALIBUT WITH LEMON BASIL VINAIGRETTE

Makes 4 servings

The vinaigrette in this recipe is also good with salmon or swordfish.

FISH

4 x 170-g (6-oz) halibut fillets
Sea salt and freshly ground black pepper

VINAIGRETTE

1 tsp grated lemon zest
2 tbsp freshly squeezed lemon juice
¼ tsp sea salt
Freshly ground black pepper
2 garlic cloves, cut in half
2 tbsp extra-virgin olive oil
3 tbsp thinly sliced fresh basil leaves
1 tbsp drained capers
115 g (4 oz) finely diced tomatoes

To make the fish: Preheat the oven to 180°C/350°F/gas 4. Lightly oil a baking dish large enough to hold the fillets in a single layer.

Season the fillets with salt and pepper. Place in the prepared baking dish. Bake for 15–18 minutes, or until the fish is opaque all the way through.

To make the vinaigrette: While the fish is baking, combine the lemon zest, lemon juice, salt and pepper to taste in a small bowl. Spear the garlic on the tines of a fork and use it to beat the lemon juice mixture. Beat in the oil and then stir in the basil, capers and tomatoes.

Place the fillets on heated plates, spoon on the vinaigrette and serve.

Per serving. Carbohydrates: 2.1 g; Protein: 35.7 g; Fat: 10.7 g; Calories/kJ: 256/1,072

SOLE WITH HORSERADISH CREAM SAUCE

Makes 4 servings

You can also use cod, salmon or halibut for this dish. Just increase the cooking time.

Note: *If you don't have a frying pan large enough to hold the fillets in a single layer, use two smaller ones.*

685 g (1½ lb) sole fillets, rinsed and patted dry
Sea salt and freshly ground black pepper
2 tbsp unsalted butter
2 tbsp thinly sliced spring onion
1 tbsp white wine vinegar
160 ml (6 fl oz) whipping cream
2 tbsp prepared horseradish
1 tbsp minced fresh parsley

Season the fillets with salt and pepper.

Heat a large frying pan over medium heat. Add the butter and watch carefully for the foaming to subside. As soon as it does, add the fillets. Cook until lightly golden. Using a wide spatula, flip the fillets over. If the fillets are very thin, remove the pan from the heat and let the residual heat finish the cooking. If not, cook for 1–2 minutes longer and remove from the pan to a plate.

Add the spring onion to the pan and stir until softened. Add the vinegar and let it bubble, then add the cream, horseradish and any juice that has accumulated around the fillets on the plate. Let the sauce simmer until thickened, about 1–2 minutes. Stir in the parsley, pour over the fillets and serve.

Per serving. Carbohydrates: 1.6 g; Protein: 31.5 g; Fat: 23.2 g; Calories/kJ: 345/1,444

PANCETTA-WRAPPED SALMON WITH RED WINE BUTTER

Makes 4 servings

Pancetta is unsmoked Italian bacon that is rolled and tied. Its taste is very similar to prosciutto. You can use prosciutto or bacon, if you prefer. This treatment can be used on other fish, such as cod or halibut.

Serve with sautéed spinach and mushrooms.

1 tbsp minced shallot
240 ml (8 fl oz) dry red wine
60 g (2 oz) unsalted butter, at room temperature
Sea salt and freshly ground black pepper
4 x 170-g (6-oz) skinless salmon fillets
1 tsp fresh thyme leaves or ½ tsp dried thyme
8 very thin pancetta slices
1 tbsp extra-virgin olive oil

Combine the shallot and wine in a small saucepan. Bring to the boil over medium-high heat. Cook until the wine is greatly reduced and turns into a syrupy glaze. Remove from the heat and pour into a small bowl. Stir in the butter until it is melted and emulsified. Season to taste with salt and pepper.

Season the salmon with salt and pepper and sprinkle with the thyme. Wrap 2 pancetta slices around each fillet.

In a frying pan large enough to hold the fillets in a single layer, heat the oil over medium heat. Add the fillets and cook until the pancetta is browned on all sides and the fillets are cooked through, about 8–10 minutes. Place the fillets on heated plates and spoon on the sauce.

Per serving. Carbohydrates: 1.2 g; Protein: 38.2 g; Fat: 39.4 g; Calories/kJ: 315/1,319

SALMON STEAKS WITH GINGER BUTTER

Makes 4 servings

This dish is simple and impressive enough for company. It is equally good made with salmon, halibut or cod fillets in place of the salmon steaks.

115 g (4 oz) unsalted butter, at room temperature
2 tbsp grated fresh ginger
3 tbsp finely chopped spring onion
Sea salt and freshly ground black pepper
4 x 230-g (8-oz) salmon steaks, 2.5-cm (1-in) thick
1 tbsp soy sauce
4 lime wedges

In a small bowl, mix the butter, ginger and spring onion. Season with salt and pepper. Remove 3 tablespoons and set aside. Wrap the remainder in plastic wrap, forming a short log. Refrigerate until ready to serve.

Place the reserved butter in a frying pan large enough to hold the steaks in a single layer. Melt over medium heat. Add the steaks and cook for about 4 minutes on each side, turning once. Add the soy sauce and give the pan a few shakes to glaze the bottom of the steaks.

Transfer the steaks, glazed side up, to heated plates or a platter. Unwrap the chilled butter and slice into 4 pieces. Top each piece of salmon with the butter and garnish with a lime wedge.

Per serving. Carbohydrates: 1.3 g; Protein: 46.2 g; Fat: 48 g; Calories/kJ: 630/2,637

QUICK PRAWNS, SCAMPI-STYLE

Makes 6 servings

Delicious served over a bed of Basic Cauliflower Mash (page 72), seasoned with goats cheese, to soak up the buttery, garlicky juices. The scampi also makes a perfect appetizer.

2 tbsp extra-virgin olive oil
4 garlic cloves, crushed
570 g (1¼ lb) large prawns, peeled and deveined
2 tbsp dry white wine
60 g (2 oz) unsalted butter, at room temperature
4 tbsp finely chopped fresh parsley
Sea salt and freshly ground black pepper

Heat the oil and garlic in a large frying pan over medium heat until the garlic starts to sizzle. Turn the heat to medium-low and cook until the garlic turns gold. Add the prawns and turn the heat back to medium.

When the prawns start to sizzle, add the wine and continue cooking – stirring occasionally – until they turn pink. Check they are cooked by taking a slice from the thick end. It should be opaque. Swirl in the butter and parsley and season to taste with salt and pepper. Serve immediately.

Per serving. Carbohydrates: 1.9 g; Protein: 19.3 g; Fat: 20.5 g; Calories/kJ: 273/1,143

SEARED TUNA WITH SOY WASABI GLAZE

Makes 4 servings

The sauce is extremely good with other fish, such as salmon and halibut. For vegetables, spinach, asparagus and mangetout are a good match with the sauce and tuna.
   Note: *Make sure your butter is cold or the sauce won't emulsify properly.*

4 x 170-g (6-oz) fresh albacore tuna steaks, about 2-cm (¾-in) thick
Vegetable oil
Sea salt and freshly ground black pepper
115 g (4 oz) cold unsalted butter
1 tbsp freshly squeezed lemon juice
3 tbsp soy sauce
1–2 tbsp prepared wasabi
3 spring onions, thinly sliced

Brush the steaks on both sides with the oil and season with salt and pepper.

Heat a heavy nonstick frying pan over high heat. Place the steaks in the pan and sear until browned. Turn over and sear the other side. Be careful not to overcook the tuna. It's best rare to medium-rare.

While the tuna is cooking, combine the butter, lemon juice, soy sauce and wasabi in a small saucepan. Heat over low heat, stirring constantly, until smooth and emulsified. Remove immediately from the heat.

Serve the tuna immediately, drenched with the sauce. Sprinkle with the spring onions.

Per serving. Carbohydrates: 2.9 g; Protein: 40.8 g; Fat: 32.7 g; Calories/kJ: 475/1,988

CLAMS STEAMED WITH BACON, GREEN OLIVES AND TOMATOES

Makes 4 servings

Before cooking clams and mussels, discard any that are open. I love this heady, punchy combination of flavours with the smoothness of the cream.

230 g (8 oz) bacon rashers, cut into 1-cm (½-in) pieces
4 garlic cloves, crushed
4 tbsp finely chopped onion
120 ml (4 fl oz) dry white wine
115 g (4 oz) drained tinned Italian plum
   tomatoes, finely chopped
12 large green olives, pitted and roughly chopped
120 ml (4 fl oz) whipping cream
1.4 kg (3 lb) clams, scrubbed
2 tbsp finely chopped fresh parsley

Cook the bacon in a large pan over low heat until crisp. Remove the bacon and discard all the fat except 1 tablespoon. Turn the heat to high and add the garlic and onion. When they sizzle, add the wine, tomatoes, olives, cream, clams and parsley.

Cover tightly and steam until the clams open, shaking the pan occasionally to redistribute the clams. When the clams have opened, add the bacon. Cover and shake a few times. Serve in heated bowls.

Per serving. Carbohydrates: 4.7 g; Protein: 13.4 g; Fat: 20.7 g; Calories/kJ: 268/1,122

MUSSELS, PIZZERIA-STYLE

Makes 4 servings

These mussels are 'all-dressed'. If you want, a little pepperoni added to the sauce would not be out of place. This recipe works with clams, too.

60 ml (2 fl oz) extra-virgin olive oil
2 tbsp finely chopped onion
4 garlic cloves, crushed
50 g (1¾ oz) thinly sliced mushrooms
1 small finely diced red or green pepper
115 g (4 oz) tinned plum tomatoes with juice, coarsely chopped
120 ml (4 fl oz) dry white wine
½ tsp dried oregano
900 g (2 lb) fresh mussels, debearded if necessary and scrubbed
Dried chilli flakes
2 tbsp finely chopped fresh parsley
30 g (1 oz) freshly grated Parmesan cheese

Heat the oil in a large pan over medium-high heat. Add the onion and garlic and sauté until the onion becomes translucent. Add the mushrooms and peppers and cook until both become soft. Add the tomatoes, wine and oregano. Bring to the boil.

Add the mussels and chilli flakes. Cover, turn up the heat and cook until the mussels open, shaking the pan occasionally. Discard any that stay closed. Stir in the parsley and cheese. Serve immediately.

Per serving. Carbohydrates: 3.6 g; Protein: 4.2 g; Fat: 15.2 g; Calories/kJ: 195/816

CHICKEN AND TURKEY

I'M STATING THE OBVIOUS HERE, because we all know that chicken is one of the most versatile meats. It's easy to prepare, cooks quickly, suits almost any seasoning and is universally beloved. Along with hard-boiled eggs, it's good to have a few cooked drumsticks, wings or breasts in your fridge as a quick meal.

For easy casseroles, add cooked boneless chicken pieces to such dishes as Spaghetti Squash Arrabbiata (page 78). Really, most any casserole, vegetable side dish, soup or salad can be enhanced by chicken.

Equally obvious: everything that applies to chicken goes double for turkey. Christmas leftovers are never a problem!

Try these other favourites to warm the hearts of family and friends.

Flat-Roasted Chicken with Prosciutto and Green Olives (page 102)

Lemongrass Chicken (page 101)

Thai BBQ Chicken Bundles (page 106)

Turkey Fillet with Pesto and Mozzarella (page 109)

CINNAMON-SPICED LEMON CHICKEN

Makes 4 servings

These chicken thighs are a perfect accompaniment to Pine Nut and Parsley Salad (page 52).

8 large bone-in chicken thighs with skin
Sea salt and freshly ground black pepper
1 tsp ground cinnamon
1 tsp ground cumin
1 tsp sweet or hot paprika
60 ml (2 fl oz) freshly squeezed lemon juice
2 tbsp extra-virgin olive oil
2 tbsp unsalted butter, cut into small pieces

Preheat the oven to 200°C/400°F/gas 6.

With a sharp knife, slash the thighs once or twice on each side. Place in a large bowl and season liberally with salt and pepper.

In a small bowl, mix the cinnamon, cumin, paprika, lemon juice and oil. Add to the chicken and toss to coat.

Place the thighs in a single layer in a baking dish. Dot with the butter. Bake for 30 minutes, basting occasionally with the butter.

Turn on the grill. Grill 10–15 cm (4–6 in) from the heat until golden brown. Serve with the pan juices.

Per serving. Carbohydrates: 1.7 g; Protein: 31.3 g; Fat: 32.3 g; Calories/kJ: 429/1,796

LEMONGRASS CHICKEN

Makes 4 servings

If you have not yet become acquainted with the flavours of Southeast Asia, this is a good introduction. Serve with Cucumber Salad with Peanuts, Coconut and Lime (page 55).

2 fresh lemongrass stalks
2 small shallots, coarsely chopped
2 garlic cloves, coarsely chopped
1 small hot chilli pepper, coarsely chopped
1 tbsp fish sauce
4 x 225-g (8-oz) boneless chicken breast halves with skin
1 tbsp vegetable oil
Sea salt and freshly ground black pepper

Remove the fibrous outer covering and top of the lemongrass and chop the tender part as finely as you can. Place in a food processor and add the shallots, garlic, chilli and fish sauce. Pulse to a fine paste.

Place the chicken in a large bowl and add the paste. Toss to coat well. Cover and refrigerate for at least 2 hours or up to overnight.

Preheat the oven to 230°C/450°F/gas 8.

Pat the chicken dry with paper towels. Heat the oil in a large ovenproof nonstick frying pan over medium-high heat. Add the chicken, skin side down, season with salt and pepper and cook until lightly browned, about 5 minutes.

Place the pan in the oven and bake for 5 minutes. Turn the chicken over and bake for an additional 5 minutes, or until cooked through.

Per serving. Carbohydrates: 2 g; Protein: 51.2 g; Fat: 16.8 g; Calories/kJ: 379/1,586

FLAT-ROASTED CHICKEN WITH PROSCIUTTO AND GREEN OLIVES

Makes 4 servings

This chicken dish will produce a wonderfully enticing aroma – especially welcoming on a chilly night.

Buy the prosciutto in a single piece, rather than sliced, and cut it into small cubes.

1 chicken, 1.6 kg–1.8 kg (3½–4 lb)
Sea salt and freshly ground black pepper
115 g (4 oz) prosciutto, cut into 1-cm (½-in) cubes
60 g (2 oz) minced shallot
2 garlic cloves, crushed
85 g (3 oz) unpitted green olives
120 ml (4 fl oz) dry white wine

Preheat the oven to 180°C/350°F/gas 4. Lightly oil a large roasting tin.

With a sharp heavy knife, split the chicken down the backbone and open it up. Turn it breast side up and flatten with the palm of your hand. Cut a slit in the skin in the centre, at the bottom of the breast area, and slip both drumstick tips through it. Sprinkle liberally with salt and pepper. Transfer the chicken, breast side down, to the prepared roasting tin. Bake for 45 minutes.

In a small bowl, mix the prosciutto, shallot, garlic and olives.

Remove the chicken from the oven and transfer to a plate. Remove any accumulated fat from the tin and discard. Scatter the prosciutto mixture evenly in the tin and add the wine. Place the chicken, skin side up, in the tin. Bake for 45 minutes longer.

Remove the chicken from the tin. Either carve the meat from the bones or cut the chicken into serving pieces. Pour the prosciutto mixture over the chicken and serve.

Per serving. Carbohydrates: 0.4 g; Protein: 52.4 g; Fat: 31.2 g; Calories/kJ: 523/2,189

CHICKEN WITH BACON, CREAM AND THYME

Makes 4 servings

Delicious served with steamed spinach and Basic Cauliflower Mash (page 72) on the side. If you don't have fresh thyme, a light sprinkling of dried thyme will do.

4 x 225-g (8-oz) boneless chicken breast halves with skin
Sea salt and freshly ground black pepper
8 bacon rashers
8 small fresh thyme sprigs
1 tbsp vegetable oil
120 ml (4 fl oz) chicken stock or water
240 ml (8 fl oz) whipping cream
1 garlic clove, crushed

Preheat the oven to 180°C/350°F/gas 4.

Lightly season the chicken with salt and pepper. Wrap 2 bacon rashers around each breast, forming an × in the middle of the skin side. Tuck 2 thyme sprigs per breast behind the bacon.

Heat the oil in an ovenproof frying pan over medium-high heat. Place the chicken breasts, bacon side down, in the pan and cook until the bacon and chicken skin are browned. Turn over and cook until the other side is browned.

Drain off the fat and add the stock or water, cream and garlic. Bring to the boil.

Transfer the pan to the oven. Bake for 15–20 minutes, or until the cream has thickened. Season to taste with salt and pepper. Let stand a few minutes before serving.

Per serving. Carbohydrates: 2.1 g; Protein: 43.7 g; Fat: 41.7 g; Calories/kJ: 565/2,365

BUTTER CHICKEN

Makes 4 servings

This recipe is from Rosebud, a member of lowcarber.org. It's simple to make and great served with Cucumber Salad with Peanuts, Coconut and Lime (page 55) and Basic Cauliflower 'Rice' (page 73) seasoned with curry powder.

Butter chicken usually requires making tandoori chicken first, but you don't have to do that with Rosebud's recipe. Just start with commercially prepared tandoori paste, which you can buy in most well-stocked supermarkets.

2 tbsp vegetable oil
685 g (1½ lb) boneless, skinless chicken breast halves, cut into bite-size pieces
2 tbsp tandoori paste
180 ml (6 fl oz) whipping cream
1 tbsp unsalted butter
2 tbsp toasted sliced almonds (optional)

Heat the oil in a large frying pan over medium-high heat. Add the chicken and cook, stirring occasionally, until lightly browned and almost cooked through, about 4–5 minutes. Stir in the tandoori paste and then add the cream. Simmer for about 5 minutes, or until the cream is lightly thickened. Stir in the butter and garnish with the almonds (if using).

Per serving. Carbohydrates: 2.7 g; Protein: 37.7 g; Fat: 43.1 g; Calories/kJ: 558/2,336

THAI BBQ CHICKEN BUNDLES

Makes 4 servings

Here's one of my favourite recipes.

*   *Be careful not to make your bundles too big or they will fall apart when you bite into them.*

1 small bunch fresh coriander
2 garlic cloves
3 tbsp fish sauce
1 tsp coarsely ground black pepper
6 x 225-g (8-oz) boneless chicken breast halves with skin
1 large head lettuce, washed and dried
½ cucumber, halved lengthwise and cut into thin half moons
1 small bunch fresh mint
Thai Sweet and Sour Chilli Dipping Sauce (page 136)
40 g (1¼ oz) unsalted roasted peanuts, chopped

Coarsely chop half of the coriander and place in a blender or food processor. Add the garlic, fish sauce and pepper. Process to a paste.

Place the chicken in a large bowl. Add the paste and toss well to coat. Cover and refrigerate for at least 2 hours or up to overnight.

Preheat the grill. Line a rimmed baking sheet with foil.

Place the chicken on the sheet, skin side down. Grill about 10–15 cm (4–6 in) from the heat for 4–5 minutes. Turn the pieces over and grill until the skin is crisp and the chicken is cooked all the way through (the juices should run clear when the thickest area is pricked with a fork).

Arrange the lettuce, cucumber and mint on a large platter. Remove the stems from the remaining coriander and add to the platter. Cut the chicken into 2-cm (¾-in) slices and place on the platter.

Divide the sauce among individual dipping bowls and sprinkle with the peanuts.

To eat, take a lettuce leaf and tear it in half. Place a few cucumber slices, a few mint and coriander leaves, and a slice or two of chicken on the leaf. Roll up into a snug bundle, dip into the sauce and eat.

Per serving (without sauce). Carbohydrates: 4.6 g; Protein: 40.4 g; Fat: 20.2 g; Calories/kJ: 372/1,557

Per 2 tbsp sauce with peanuts. Carbohydrates: 1.6 g; Protein: 0.5 g; Fat: 0 g; Calories/kJ: 8/33

15 WAYS TO DRESS UP CHICKEN

There are times when we want something fast but tasty, and most low-carbers fall back on boneless, skinless chicken breasts. Here are some quick ways to give them extra oomph. Just top the cooked meat as directed and, if needed, grill until heated through.

A la grecque Top with feta cheese, black olives, tomatoes and onions.

Bistro Apply caramelized onions and Brie; grill until the cheese melts.

Blue moon Cover with blue cheese and sautéed mushrooms. Grill until melted, then serve with lettuce and tomato.

Caprese Arrange sliced tomatoes and sliced mozzarella on top. Serve with mayonnaise enhanced with Basil Pesto (page 134).

De-lox Spread with cream cheese and top with smoked salmon, avocado and thin slices of red onion.

Gingersnap Use a dipping sauce of soy sauce, ginger, toasted sesame oil, sweetener and spring onion.

Madame Top with sliced smoked turkey and Dijon mustard; add Gruyère cheese and grill until melted.

Milanese Coat with finely grated Parmesan cheese and oregano before cooking.

Olivada Top with Mushroom Tapenade (page 30) and serve with Broccoli Italianissimo (page 69).

Provence Spread with goats cheese and sprinkle with walnuts and crisp bacon.

Holsteiner Top with a fried egg – add bacon and you have breakfast!

Stroganoff Mix sautéed mushrooms and onions with soured cream and spoon over the top.

Sushi Dab with mayo mixed with wasabi; top with cucumber, avocado and crab.

Thai Spread with some natural peanut butter and sprinkle with matchsticks of cucumber; wrap in a lettuce leaf.

Turkish Toss together garlic, parsley, olive oil, paprika and artichoke hearts; spoon on top and serve with yogurt or soured cream.

OVEN-FRIED CHICKEN

Makes 6 servings

Move over, Colonel Sanders! The secret to success here is baking the chicken on a wire rack set in a shallow pan.

150 g (5½ oz) pork rinds
6 bone-in chicken thighs with skin
6 bone-in chicken legs with skin
1 large egg
120 ml (4 fl oz) mayonnaise
2 tbsp Dijon mustard
1½ tsp dried thyme
1 tsp sea salt
1 tsp freshly ground black pepper
1 tsp dried oregano
½ tsp garlic powder

Preheat the oven to 200°C/400°F/gas 6. Place a wire cooling rack in a large rimmed baking sheet.

In a food processor, grind the pork rinds. (A few larger pieces are desirable. I like to squish them up in a bag first to get the process started.) Spread on a large plate.

Remove the skin from the chicken pieces. (Using a paper towel to grip the skin helps.)

In a shallow bowl, mix the egg, mayonnaise, mustard, thyme, salt, pepper, oregano and garlic powder. Dip each piece of chicken in the mayonnaise mixture to coat thoroughly and then roll in the pork rinds to cover completely. Place the chicken on the wire rack, making sure there is enough room around each piece for the chicken to roast evenly and crisply.

Bake for 40 minutes, or until the juice runs clear when the thickest part of the thigh is pricked with a knife.

Per serving. Carbohydrates: 0.9 g; Protein: 52.8 g; Fat: 46.9 g; Calories/kJ: 650/2,721

TURKEY FILLET WITH PESTO AND SMOKED MOZZARELLA

Makes 6 servings

Leftovers are fabulous! If you want to dress this up a bit, serve it with Tomato Garlic Cream Sauce (page 135).

Other types of smoked cheese can be used if you can't find smoked mozzarella, such as Cheddar or provolone. If you don't have homemade pesto, commercially prepared is fine.

6 turkey fillets, about 900 g (2 lb) in total
Sea salt and freshly ground black pepper
120 ml (4 fl oz) Basil Pesto (page 134)
115 g (4 oz) thinly sliced smoked mozzarella cheese, cut into 1-cm (½-in) strips

Preheat the oven to 180°C/350°F/gas 4.

Cut each fillet lengthwise almost in half and open like a book. Sprinkle with salt and pepper. Using half of the pesto, spread it evenly on one side of each of the fillets. Place the cheese evenly on top of the pesto, and fold the fillets closed.

With toothpicks, skewer each fillet on the cut side to secure. Brush the fillets with the remaining pesto. Transfer to a rimmed baking sheet.

Bake for 20 minutes, or until cooked through (if you use smaller fillets remember to reduce the cooking time accordingly). Slice the fillets crosswise into 2.5-cm (1-in) rounds and arrange on a serving platter. Serve with the pan juices poured on top.

Per serving. Carbohydrates: 1.4 g; Protein: 44.6 g; Fat: 16.2 g; Calories/kJ: 342/1,432

PORK, BEEF AND LAMB

ONE OF THE BEST THINGS ABOUT BEING A LOW-CARBER is that you can enjoy meat without feeling guilty.

Pork is one of my favourite meats. There is nothing more succulent or satisfying than tender ribs that fall off the bone. Just thinking of all the luscious preparations that are made with pork – prosciutto, salami, ham, bacon, sausages, pâté – is enough to make me swoon. My first ever rack of lamb had much the same effect. But as well as elegant preparations, lamb is great with exotic flavours – just try Moroccan-Style Lamb Stew (page 123).

Beef was a near-taboo subject for many years, almost eclipsed by the boneless, skinless chicken breast, but even through those – ahem – 'lean' times I have always enjoyed a big steak.

Here are some more of my favourite meat dishes.

Pizza Quiche with Garlic Sausage (page 115)
Pork Loin Steaks with Lemon Thyme Cream (page 113)
Grilled Rump Steak with Cumin Aioli (page 122)
Coriander Lamb with Tomato Vinaigrette (page 124)

RIBS WITH QUICK BBQ GLAZE

Makes 2 racks of ribs

This is an easy method for making very tender ribs. After an initial baking, glaze the ribs with this quick barbecue sauce and grill them until browned. You can also bake the ribs in advance and then glaze them later.

Note: Liquid smoke can be found in the speciality section of good supermarkets or in some delicatessens. If you can't find any, don't worry – it isn't essential.

RIBS

2 racks pork back ribs
Sea salt

GLAZE

2 tbsp tomato purée
2 tbsp mayonnaise
1 tsp Worcestershire sauce
1 tbsp soy sauce
⅛ tsp liquid smoke
½ tsp garlic powder
2 tsp Splenda

To make the ribs: Preheat the oven to 120°C/250°F/gas ½.

Place the ribs on a piece of heavy-duty foil and sprinkle lightly with salt. Close the foil over the ribs, forming a loose tent, and crimp the edges securely. Place on a rimmed baking sheet.

Bake for 1½–2 hours. You can let the ribs cool at this point for finishing later or glaze them and grill immediately.

To make the glaze: In a small bowl, mix the tomato purée, mayonnaise, Worcestershire sauce, soy sauce, liquid smoke, garlic powder and sweetener.

Preheat the grill and position the rack 20 cm (8 in) from the heat.

Open the foil and pour off the liquid. Using the back of a spoon, liberally apply the glaze to one side of the ribs. Grill until bubbly with a few darkened spots. Turn the ribs over and apply the remaining glaze. Grill again until browned and bubbly.

Per serving. Carbohydrates: 4 g; Protein: 76 g; Fat: 37 g; Calories/kJ: 670/2,805
Per serving (sauce only). Carbohydrates: 4.2 g; Protein: 1.7 g; Fat: 11.2 g; Calories/kJ: 123/515

PORK LOIN STEAKS WITH LEMON THYME CREAM

Makes 4 servings

This takes very little time once you start cooking and is perfect for company.

3 tbsp freshly squeezed lemon juice
1 tbsp chopped fresh thyme or 1 tsp dried thyme
2 tsp grated lemon rind
2 garlic cloves, crushed
¼ tsp sea salt
8 x 1-cm (½-in) boneless pork loin steaks, about 100 g (3 oz) each
1 tbsp unsalted butter
240 ml (8 fl oz) whipping cream
Freshly ground black pepper

In a large bowl, mix the lemon juice, thyme, lemon rind, garlic and ¼ teaspoon salt. Add the pork and toss to coat with the mixture. Cover and refrigerate for at least 1 hour or up to overnight.

Melt the butter in a large frying pan over medium-high heat. Remove the pork from the marinade and place the pieces flat in the pan. (Work in batches if necessary.) Fry on both sides, turning once, until browned.

Return the pork to the pan and add any marinade remaining in the bowl. Add the cream and bring to the boil. Turn down to a simmer and cook until the cream thickens. Season to taste with salt and pepper.

Per serving. Carbohydrates: 3.1 g; Protein: 37 g; Fat: 29 g; Calories/kJ: 429/1,796

PIZZA QUICHE WITH GARLIC SAUSAGE

Makes 8 servings

This recipe is from Donald – a low-carber who has lost 45 kg (100 lb).

Donald cuts the quiche into pieces and then freezes them to take to work for lunch. Of course, you can use any pizza toppings that you prefer. The mushrooms and sausage are my preference. This is one of the most popular recipes ever from lowcarber.org.

115 g (4 oz) cream cheese, at room temperature
4 large eggs
80 ml (3 fl oz) whipping cream
30 g (1 oz) freshly grated Parmesan cheese
1 tbsp finely chopped fresh chives
½ tsp crushed garlic
½ tsp dried oregano
100 g (3½ oz) grated Asiago cheese (if unavailable use Parmesan)
230 g (8 oz) grated full-fat mozzarella cheese
120 ml (4 fl oz) passata (sieved tomatoes)
145 g (5 oz) sliced mushrooms, sautéed
2 pork sausages with garlic, casings removed, crumbled and cooked

Preheat the oven to 180°C/350°F/gas 4. Butter a 32.5- × 22.5-cm (13- × 9-in) shallow baking dish.

In a food processor, blend together the cream cheese and eggs until smooth. Add the cream, 30 g (1 oz) Parmesan, chives, garlic and oregano. Blend until smooth.

Scatter the Asiago and half of the mozzarella in the prepared baking dish. Pour the egg mixture over the cheese. Bake for 30 minutes.

Spread with the tomato sauce. Scatter the mushrooms and sausage over the top. Cover with the remaining mozzarella.

Turn on the grill and grill about 15 cm (6 in) from the heat until brown and bubbly. Let stand for 5 minutes or so before cutting.

Per serving. Carbohydrates: 3.5 g; Protein: 16.3 g; Fat: 25 g; Calories/kJ: 305/1,277

PORK AND SHIITAKE MUSHROOM MEATBALLS

Makes 24 meatballs

These taste a lot like the inside of a wonton. Like all meatballs, they are good cold and make a great appetizer. Serve with soy sauce mixed with vinegar and sweetener to taste or Thai Sweet and Sour Chilli Dipping Sauce (page 136).

I like adding these meatballs to chicken stock with some finely shredded cabbage and ginger and eating as a soup.

10 medium dried shiitake mushrooms
900 g (2 lb) minced pork
2 tbsp soy sauce
1 tsp sea salt
1 tsp Splenda
2 spring onions, finely chopped
1 tsp toasted sesame oil
2 large eggs

Place the mushrooms in a bowl and cover them with boiling water. Let stand until completely soft, about 30 minutes. Squeeze the water out of the mushrooms with your hands, remove the tough stems, and chop finely. Place in a large bowl.

Add the pork, soy sauce, salt, sweetener, spring onion, oil and eggs. Mix until everything is well-combined.

Bring a large pan of water to the boil. Shape the mixture into 24 meatballs, using 2 tablespoons for each. Drop the meatballs gently into the water. When the water returns to the boil, cover the pan, turn down the heat to a simmer and cook gently for 15 minutes. Remove with a slotted spoon.

Per meatball. Carbohydrates: 1.2 g; Protein: 7 g; Fat: 10.6 g; Calories/kJ: 131/548

SHEPHERD'S PIE WITH MUSHROOMS, SMOKED CHEDDAR, BACON AND SOURED CREAM

Makes 9 servings

The smoked Cheddar is great, but regular Cheddar will do. This is fabulous for breakfast!

BEEF

1.3 kg (3 lb) lean minced beef
1 large onion, finely diced
2 large sticks celery, finely diced
¼ tsp dried thyme or ½ tsp fresh thyme leaves
1 tbsp tomato purée
Sea salt and freshly ground black pepper
2 tbsp unsalted butter
230 g (8 oz) mushrooms, coarsely chopped

CAULIFLOWER PURÉE

900 g (2 lb) cauliflower, trimmed
230 g (8 oz) grated smoked Cheddar cheese
60 ml (2 fl oz) soured cream
2 tbsp unsalted butter
1 large egg
8 bacon rashers, cooked until crisp then crumbled
Paprika

To make the beef: Place the beef in a large pan and cook over high heat, crumbling the meat with a spoon until it loses its raw, red colour. Stir in the onion, celery, thyme and tomato purée. Season lightly with salt and pepper. Cover tightly, turn the heat to low and cook for 20 minutes, stirring occasionally. Add a touch of water if the mixture looks too dry; it should look juicy but not wet.

Heat the butter in a large frying pan over high heat until the foam subsides. Add mushrooms and cook briskly until the water has evaporated and the mushrooms are soft. Add the mushrooms to the beef mixture and cook for 10 minutes longer.

To make the cauliflower purée: Chop the cauliflower, including the core, into chunks. Place in a large pot and add enough water to cover the pieces by 2.5 cm (1 in). Bring to the boil over high heat and cook until extremely tender, about 20 minutes. Drain well. Transfer to a food processor and blend until smooth. Remove about a cup of the purée and stir into the beef.

To the remaining cauliflower in the food processor, add the cheese, soured cream and butter; blend well. Add the egg and blend until smooth. Add the bacon and pulse once or twice to combine.

Preheat the oven to 180°C/350°F/gas 4.

Spread the beef mixture in a 22.5- × 22.5-cm (9- × 9-in) deep baking dish. Cover with the cauliflower mixture and smooth the top. Sprinkle with the paprika or make crisscross lines, dots or whatever strikes your fancy. Place the baking dish on a large rimmed baking sheet to catch any drips.

Bake for 45 minutes, or until bubbly and browned. Let the pie stand for 10 minutes before serving.

Per serving. Carbohydrates: 5.8 g; Protein: 42.9 g; Fat: 29.5 g; Calories/kJ: 475/1,988

CAULIFLOWER CHAMELEON

There is no other vegetable in the low-carb repertoire that is as versatile as cauliflower. It can be stir-fried, mashed, roasted, and more. It's obvious salad material and a less-obvious thickener for gravies, soups or sauces.

It's also low in carbohydrate and has more potassium than many supplements.

BOLOGNESE LASAGNE

Makes 8 servings

In my former life, Bolognese was the *lasagne. But it gave me bedtime indigestion so bad that I stopped eating it. Thank goodness for this recipe – no indigestion, it's good cold and reheats wonderfully!*

685 g (1½ lb) ricotta cheese
2 large eggs
⅛ tsp freshly grated nutmeg
½ tsp sea salt
60 g (2 oz) freshly grated Parmesan cheese
720 ml (26 fl oz) Bolognese Sauce (page 130) or meat sauce, warmed
Lasagne Noodles (page 84)
170 g (6 oz) grated full-fat mozzarella cheese

In a medium bowl, mix the ricotta, eggs, nutmeg, salt and Parmesan. Cover and refrigerate for up to 1 day.

Spread one-quarter of the sauce in a 32.5- × 22.5-cm (13- × 9-in) baking dish. Carefully transfer 1 lasagne noodle to the dish. Spread with another quarter of the sauce. Evenly spread the ricotta filling on top.

Add more sauce, the remaining lasagne noodle and the rest of the sauce.

Bake for 35 minutes. Sprinkle with the mozzarella and bake for 10 minutes longer. Remove from the oven and let rest for 10 minutes before serving.

Per serving. Carbohydrates: 10.5 g; Protein: 49.8 g; Fat: 75.7 g; Calories/kJ: 942/3,943

GRILLED RUMP STEAK WITH CUMIN AIOLI

Makes 6 servings

You can use a sirloin steak in place of the rump steak. In fact, any steak is good with the cumin aioli. Rump steak is best served medium-rare, and leftovers are wonderful.

CUMIN AIOLI

1 tbsp cumin seeds
1 large egg
1 tsp Dijon mustard
½ tsp sea salt
1 garlic clove, crushed
120 ml (4 fl oz) vegetable oil
4 tsp freshly squeezed lemon juice
120 ml (4 fl oz) extra-virgin olive oil

STEAK

3 tbsp extra-virgin olive oil
½ tsp sea salt
2 garlic cloves, crushed
½ tsp freshly ground black pepper
1.1 kg (2½ lb) rump steak

To make the cumin aioli: Place the cumin seeds in a small frying pan and stir over medium heat for 2 minutes, or until they darken a shade. Remove from the heat. Finely grind half of the cumin seeds in a coffee grinder or with a mortar and pestle.

In a blender or food processor, combine the egg, mustard, salt, garlic and the ground cumin seeds. Process briefly to blend. With the motor running, add the vegetable oil in a slow, steady stream. Pour in the lemon juice and then slowly add the olive oil until the aioli is emulsified. If the mixture seems too thick, add a spoonful or two of water. Scrape the aioli into a bowl and stir in the whole cumin seeds. Cover and refrigerate.

To make the steak: In a small bowl, mix the oil, salt, garlic and pepper. Spread on both sides of the steak. Cover and refrigerate up to overnight.

Preheat the grill. Grill the steak for 3–4 minutes on each side for medium-rare. Remove the steak from the heat and let it stand for a few minutes. Slice very thinly across the grain and serve with the aioli on the side.

Per serving. Carbohydrates: 1.2 g; Protein: 42.7 g; Fat: 58 g; Calories/kJ: 701/2,934

MOROCCAN-STYLE LAMB STEW

Makes 4 servings

This stew is great on a cold day, and leftovers are even better! I think lamb shoulder makes the best stewing meat. Serve with Basic Cauliflower 'Rice' (page 73).

2 tbsp extra-virgin olive oil
1 large onion, finely chopped
3 cloves garlic, crushed
900 g (2 lb) stewing lamb
½ tsp sea salt
½ tsp ground ginger
½ tsp freshly ground black pepper
½ tsp ground cinnamon
¼ tsp ground allspice
360 ml (13 fl oz) water
2 tbsp finely chopped fresh parsley
2 tbsp finely chopped fresh coriander
1–2 tbsp freshly squeezed lemon juice

Heat the oil in a large heavy pan over medium-heat. Add the onion and garlic and cook until the onion is lightly browned, about 5 minutes.

Stir in the lamb, salt, ginger, pepper, cinnamon, allspice, water, parsley and coriander. Bring to the boil. Turn down to a bare simmer, cover and cook until the lamb is tender, about 1½ to 2 hours; replenish the water if necessary. Add the lemon juice and adjust the seasoning.

Per serving. Carbohydrates: 4.6 g; Protein: 56.2 g; Fat: 63.1 g; Calories/kJ: 826/3,458

CORIANDER LAMB WITH TOMATO VINAIGRETTE

Makes 4 servings

VINAIGRETTE

2 medium ripe tomatoes, seeded and chopped
3 tbsp white wine vinegar
2 garlic cloves, crushed
120 ml (4 fl oz) extra-virgin olive oil
2 tbsp coriander leaves, coarsely chopped

LAMB

900 g (2 lb) boneless leg of lamb
3 tbsp coriander seeds
2 garlic cloves, crushed
90 ml (3 fl oz) extra-virgin olive oil
Sea salt and freshly ground black pepper
1 small red onion, cut into 8 wedges

To make the vinaigrette: In a blender or food processor, combine the tomatoes, vinegar and garlic. Process until smooth. With the motor running, slowly drizzle in the oil. Add the coriander and pulse to combine. Cover and refrigerate.

To make the lamb: Trim the fat and sinew from the lamb and cut into 2.5-cm (1-in) cubes. Place in a large bowl.

Place the coriander seeds in a small frying pan. Stir over medium-heat for a few minutes, until fragrant. Cool and grind coarsely with a mortar and pestle. Transfer to a bowl and stir in the garlic and 3 tablespoons of the oil. Season to taste with salt and pepper. Add to the lamb and toss well to coat. Cover and refrigerate for at least 2 hours or up to overnight.

Heat the remaining oil in a large heavy frying pan over high heat until almost smoking. Add the lamb and onion. Toss and stir until browned on the outside and medium-rare on the inside, 4–5 minutes. Serve with the vinaigrette on the side.

Per serving. Carbohydrates: 5.8 g; Protein: 40.6 g; Fat: 69.9 g; Calories/kJ: 821/3,437

MOUSSAKA

Makes 10 servings

I love the flavour of lamb with tomatoes and cinnamon. And it makes the kitchen smell utterly delicious. Serve the moussaka with a Greek salad or fried courgettes (zucchinis) with garlic, lemon and oregano.

Moussaka is a great dish to feed a crowd, and the leftovers are perfect for breakfast! You can also try it with beef.

AUBERGINE

2 x 455 g (1 lb) aubergines
120 ml (4 fl oz) extra-virgin olive oil

LAMB

2 tbsp extra-virgin olive oil
1 medium onion, finely chopped
2 garlic cloves, crushed
1.3 kg (3 lb) lean minced lamb
240 ml (8 fl oz) tinned Italian plum tomatoes,
    well-drained and finely chopped
1 tsp sea salt
1 tsp ground cinnamon
1 tsp dried oregano
3 large eggs
100 g (3½ oz) freshly grated Parmesan cheese

SAUCE

500 g (1 lb 2 oz) ricotta cheese
60 g (2 oz) freshly grated Parmesan cheese
30 g (1 oz) finely grated Pecorino Romano cheese
¼ tsp freshly grated nutmeg
¼ tsp sea salt
Freshly ground black pepper
3 large eggs

To make the aubergine: Preheat the grill.

Trim the stem end from the aubergines and slice lengthwise into 8-mm (⅓-in) slices. Brush both sides with the oil and place on rimmed baking sheets. Grill 10 cm (4 in) from the heat until browned on one side. Turn over and brown the other side.

To make the lamb: Heat the oil in a large pan over medium-high heat. Add the onion and garlic and sauté until the onion browns slightly. Add the lamb and cook over high heat, breaking up lumps with a spoon, until the meat loses its raw look. (I find a hand-held blender comes in handy to do this, after the meat is cooked.)

Add the tomatoes, salt, cinnamon and oregano. Cook at a simmer for 30 minutes. Remove from the heat and let cool. Beat in the eggs and cheese.

To make the sauce: In a medium bowl, mix the ricotta, Parmesan, Pecorino Romano, nutmeg, salt and pepper. Beat in the eggs.

To assemble: Preheat the oven to 180°C/350°F/gas 4.

Place a layer of aubergine (without overlapping the slices) in a 32.5- × 22.5-cm (13- × 9-in) glass baking dish. Spoon half of the meat in an even layer over the aubergine. Top with another layer of aubergine and then the remaining meat. Place the remaining aubergine on top and cover with the sauce, spreading it out evenly.

Bake for 45 minutes to 1 hour, until the top is golden brown. Let stand for at least 10 minutes before cutting.

Per serving. Carbohydrates: 7.4 g; Protein: 42.6 g; Fat: 46.6 g; Calories/kJ: 633/2,650

SAUCES AND CONDIMENTS

IN THE SAME WAY THAT VEGETABLES CAN MAKE A MEAL, so can sauces. A plain piece of meat and a plain vegetable need never be boring if you have a few tricks up your sleeve. A simple pan sauce is a good basic to be comfortable with – try the Basic Herb and Wine Pan Sauce on page 131. After you have finished cooking meat or fish in a frying pan, place the food on a plate and keep warm. Drain off most of the fat and add a splash of wine, stock or water to the pan. Bring to the boil, scraping the bottom of the pan to release the flavourful brown bits, then add a splash of whipping cream and boil until thickened. Believe it or not, you can also blend liquids like soy sauce or citrus juice into commercially prepared mayonnaise and heat it for a warm sauce. You can also melt cheese into mayo for a quickie cheese sauce or blend in a combination of water and cream for a more creamy sauce. Or try one of these recipes.

Almond and Parsley Pesto (page 132)

Thai Sweet and Sour Chilli Dipping Sauce (page 136)

Tomato Garlic Cream Sauce (page 135)

Aioli (page 139)

BOLOGNESE SAUCE

Makes about 1.5 litres (2½ pints)

It's great to have your own meat sauce on hand for quick meals. It can be tossed with cooked cauliflower, cabbage or spaghetti squash and cheese. You can even pour it on a salad or use it as a dip.

Since this sauce simmers for several hours, it's worth making in quantity.

2 tbsp unsalted butter
½ small onion, finely chopped
1 small celery stick, finely chopped
900 g (2 lb) lean minced beef or beef and pork
240 ml (8 fl oz) dry white wine
4 x 400 g(14 oz) tins Italian plum tomatoes with juice, finely chopped
1½ tsp sea salt
240 ml (8 fl oz) whipping cream

Melt the butter in a large heavy pan over medium heat. Add the onion and celery and cook until soft but not brown, about 5 minutes. Add the meat and raise the heat. Cook, crumbling the meat into small pieces with a spoon, until browned.

Add the wine and cook until it evaporates. Add the tomatoes and salt, bring to the boil, and turn down to a simmer. Cook for at least 3 hours, stirring from time to time. (Cooking for 4–5 hours is not out of line.) The sauce should be thick but not too thick to pour.

Add the cream and simmer for 30 minutes longer. Adjust the seasoning.

Per 120 ml (4 fl oz). Carbohydrates: 4.8 g; Protein: 15 g; Fat: 25 g; Calories/kJ: 333/1,394

BASIC HERB AND WINE PAN SAUCE

Makes 4 servings

Rosemary, thyme, dill and tarragon are all good in this sauce, but really any herb that complements the food will work. If using soft herbs like dill, basil or parsley, increase the amount to 1 tablespoon.

Use white wine for a lighter sauce and red wine for a dark one. There's nothing wrong with a red wine sauce on fish!

3 tbsp very finely chopped shallot or spring onion (white part only)
1 tbsp red wine or white wine
180 ml (6 fl oz) chicken stock
1 tsp very finely chopped fresh herbs
60 g (2 oz) cold unsalted butter, cut into cubes
Sea salt and freshly ground black pepper

Remove from the pan whatever meat or fish you cooked and place it on a plate. Cover with foil to keep warm.

Discard all but 1 tablespoon of the fat in the pan. Turn the heat to medium. Add the shallot or spring onion and sauté until softened, about 2 minutes. Add the wine and stock.

Use a spoon or metal spatula to scrape up any browned bits clinging to the bottom of the pan. Bring to the boil and cook until the liquid is reduced by half. Stir in the herbs.

Remove the pan from the heat. Stirring constantly, swirl in the butter until emulsified. Season to taste with salt and pepper.

Per serving. Carbohydrates: 1.8 g; Protein: 0.4 g; Fat: 11.1 g; Calories/kJ: 111/465

ALMOND AND PARSLEY PESTO

Makes about 240 ml (8 fl oz)

This combination is great for chicken, fish and vegetables. It's even good on tomatoes.

75 g (2½ oz) whole unblanched almonds
60 g (2 oz) fresh parsley leaves
1 garlic clove, crushed
90 ml (3 fl oz) extra-virgin olive oil
30 g (1 oz) freshly grated Parmesan cheese
Sea salt and freshly ground black pepper

Preheat the oven to 180°C/350°F/gas 4. Spread the almonds on a baking sheet and bake for 8–10 minutes, until the nuts are lightly toasted. Cool.

Combine the almonds, parsley, garlic and oil in a food processor and blend until pasty, scraping down the sides of the bowl as needed. Pulse in the cheese and season to taste with salt and pepper.

Per 1 tbsp. Carbohydrates: 0.6 g; Protein: 1.5 g; Fat: 7.6 g; Calories/kJ: 76/

FLAVOURED BUTTERS

Flavoured butters are a great way to give a little oomph to meats and vegetables. Mix seasonings into softened butter, shape the mixture into a cylinder using plastic wrap and chill. Cut slices and let them melt on top of the meats or vegetables. Here a few suggestions for flavour combinations.

Blue cheese and walnut for beef

Orange rind and basil for chicken, fish or broccoli and asparagus

Pine nut, lemon rind, basil and garlic for fish, vegetables and chicken

Sun-dried tomato, feta and oregano for chicken, pork or lamb

Rosemary, lemon and garlic for chicken, pork or lamb

Ginger, spring onion, toasted sesame oil and seeds for anything!

Prepared horseradish and chives for beef or fish

BASIL PESTO

Makes about 350 ml (12 fl oz)

A spoonful of pesto goes well with almost anything. It's great on fish, in soup as a garnish, or stirred into cream cheese or mayonnaise as a dip or dressing.

Note: *You can freeze the pesto in ice cube trays, transfer it to a plastic bag and use just a cube as needed.*

1 garlic clove, crushed
2 tbsp freshly grated Parmesan cheese
60 g (2 oz) fresh basil leaves
½ tsp sea salt
120 ml (4 fl oz) extra-virgin olive oil
30 g (1 oz) pine nuts (optional)

Place the garlic, cheese, basil, salt and oil in a food processor. Pulse until the basil is finely chopped (but don't pulverize it to death or the lovely flavour will be lost). Add the pine nuts (if using) and pulse again until the pine nuts are barely detectable.

Per 1 tbsp. Carbohydrates: 0.2 g; Protein: 0.7 g; Fat: 5.5 g; Calories/kJ: 52/218

SIMPLE TOMATO SAUCE

Makes about 350 ml (12 fl oz)

Although there are many good tomato sauces available that fit in with low-carb eating, it's great to know how to make your own.

2 tbsp extra-virgin olive oil
½ small onion, finely diced
400 g (14 oz) tin Italian plum tomatoes, well-drained and finely chopped
Sea salt and freshly ground black pepper

Heat the oil in a heavy pan over medium heat. Add the onion and sauté until translucent. Add the tomatoes and cook at a lively simmer until the sauce has reduced and the oil starts to float to the top. Season to taste with salt and pepper.

Per 60 ml (2 fl oz). Carbohydrates: 3.9 g; Protein: 1.2 g; Fat: 4.5 g; Calories/kJ: 71/297

TOMATO GARLIC CREAM SAUCE

Makes about 240 ml (8 fl oz)

This sauce goes well with prawns, scallops, white fish, pork or chicken.

1 tbsp unsalted butter
2 garlic cloves, crushed
80 ml (3 fl oz) dry white wine or dry white vermouth
2 tbsp tomato purée
240 ml (8 fl oz) chicken stock
120 ml (4 fl oz) whipping cream
Sea salt and freshly ground black pepper

Melt the butter in a small saucepan over medium heat. Add the garlic and cook until it sizzles. Add the wine or vermouth and boil until it reduces to a glaze.

Whisk in the tomato purée, stock and cream. Boil until the sauce is reduced by about half and slightly thickened. Season to taste with salt and pepper.

Per 1 tbsp. Carbohydrates: 0.7 g; Protein: 0.6 g; Fat: 3.6 g; Calories/kJ: 41/172

THAI SWEET AND SOUR CHILLI DIPPING SAUCE

Makes about 350 ml (12 fl oz)

The fans of this sauce are legion. It turns any plain meat into a Thai New Year celebration and is the very special guest of the Thai BBQ Chicken Bundles (page 106). It's traditionally served with chopped roasted peanuts on top.

Note: Xanthan gum – which provides structure and texture – can be found in good supermarkets and health food shops.

4 tbsp Splenda
240 ml (8 fl oz) water
½ red pepper, stem removed but seeds and core left in
1–3 fresh chilli peppers
2 garlic cloves, roughly chopped
1 tsp sea salt
60 ml (2 fl oz) freshly squeezed lemon juice or lime juice
3 tbsp fish sauce
1 tsp xanthan gum (see page 151)

In a cup, mix the sweetener and water.

Roughly chop the pepper and chillies. Place in a food processor or blender and add the garlic, salt, and 60 ml (2 fl oz) of the sweetened water. Blend until smooth. (The pepper seeds will remain whole.)

Add the lemon or lime juice, fish sauce and the remaining water. Pulse a few times to combine. Sprinkle the xanthan gum evenly over the surface of the liquid and blend until thickened. Cover and refrigerate for up to 1 week.

Per 2 tbsp. Carbohydrates: 1.6 g; Protein: 0.5 g; Fat: 0 g; Calories/kJ: 8/33

CRANBERRY SAUCE

Makes about 1 litre (1¾ pints)

Cranberries are rich in natural pectin and thicken just fine without sugar. The alcohol gives the sauce a wonderful rich flavour. Add more to taste, if you like.

455 g (1 lb) fresh cranberries
360 ml (12 fl oz) water
2 orange rind strips
2 lime rind strips
1 cinnamon stick
6 cloves
16 tbsp Splenda
2 tbsp cognac or bourbon (optional)

In a large saucepan over medium-high heat, bring the cranberries, water, orange rind, lime rind, cinnamon and cloves to the boil. Boil until the berry skins pop open (about 5 minutes). Remove from the heat. Add the sweeteners and cognac or bourbon (if using). Mix to thoroughly combine. Chill before serving.

Per 1 tbsp. Carbohydrates: 1 g; Protein: 0 g; Fat: 0 g;
Calories/kJ: 5/21

MAYONNAISE BY MACHINE

Makes about 300 ml (½ pint)

I remember the first time I made mayonnaise – I was all of 18 years old. It was tense and joy-filled at the same time. After painstakingly whisking in the oil drop by drop, I had my reward. It seemed like a miracle that a few ingredients could combine to make something greater than the parts.

One thing that surprises many is reading the label on the trusty jar of mayo and finding that sugar is an ingredient. The amount is not enough to cause any harm.

While I am a big fan of commercially prepared mayonnaise, there is something about making your own that is fulfilling and comforting at the same time. A food processor or blender makes the job nearly foolproof. You can also use a hand-held blender and beat the ingredients in a bowl.

Your mayonnaise may curdle if the oil is added too quickly. If this happens, place 1 egg yolk in the food processor or blender and add 1 tsp mustard. Very slowly, beat in the curdled mayonnaise. If it is too thick at any point, add a bit of warm water to thin it out. When you are halfway through, it is safe to add the curdled mixture more quickly.

1 large egg, at room temperature
1 large egg yolk, at room temperature
1–2 tsp Dijon mustard
¼ tsp sea salt
240 ml (8 fl oz) extra-virgin olive oil or vegetable oil
1 tbsp warm water
5–6 tsp freshly squeezed lemon juice

In a food processor or blender, combine the egg, egg yolk, mustard and salt. Blend to mix. With the motor running, blend in 80 ml (3 fl oz) of the oil *very* slowly – practically a drop at a time.

When the mixture starts to thicken, add the water. Then add the remaining oil in a slow, steady stream. When all the oil is incorporated, blend in the lemon juice. Taste and adjust the seasoning with more lemon juice, mustard and salt as needed.

Per 1 tbsp. Carbohydrates: 0.2 g; Protein: 0.1 g; Fat: 9.4 g; Calories/kJ: 85/356

AIOLI (GARLIC MAYONNAISE)

Makes 300–350 ml (10–12 fl oz)

This French mayonnaise gives a lift to almost any meat, fish or vegetable dish.

Mayonnaise by Machine (opposite)
3 garlic cloves, crushed

Prepare the mayonnaise as directed, adding the garlic at the end.

Per 1 tbsp. Carbohydrates: 0.3 g; Protein: 1 g; Fat: 10.7 g; Calories/kJ: 100/419

SPICE UP YOUR MAYONNAISE!

Mayonnaise makes an ideal sauce or accompaniment to all kinds of foods. It can be thinned down with water to make it easy to pour – think salad dressing. Or you can fold whipped cream into it to make it lighter and fluffier.

Adding a little spice to mayonnaise can turn a plain meal into a feast. Here are a few suggestions.

Blended basil, garlic and grated Parmesan cheese – or a spoonful of pesto

Chopped coriander, lime juice and puréed avocado

Curry powder

Dijon mustard

Grated ginger, toasted sesame seeds and soy sauce

Grated lemon, lime or orange rind

Grated or prepared horseradish

Finely chopped chillies and cumin seeds

Finely chopped oil-packed sun-dried tomatoes

Prepared wasabi paste and a touch of soy sauce

Tarragon and minced shallots

DESSERTS

YES, YES, I KNOW THAT SOME PEOPLE CAN EAT SWEETS EVERY DAY and still do fine with low-carbing. As a former sugar junkie, I know all too well the perils of sugar. These recipes use Splenda (sucralose) which is zero-calorie, low-carb and, unlike some other sweeteners, does not break down when heated.

My humble opinion is that sweets should be kept for an occasional treat. They're best saved for a special occasion, perhaps a dinner party where you want to impress your non-low-carb – or low-carb – friends. Making a daily habit of treats is a habit that you may have to break down the road, and that's no fun at all!

But when you do indulge, enjoy desserts to the hilt. Here are some of my favourites.

Strawberry Shortcakes with Mascarpone Balsamic Cream (page 148)

Vanilla Panna Cotta (page 158)

Tiramisu (page 159)

Pumpkin Tart (page 156)

THE SWEET TRUTH

There aren't too many times when it's better to reject the real deal in favour of something fake. But if you want something sweet and you *don't* want sugar, you have a few options to consider.

Everyone has an opinion on artificial sweeteners – which are good for you, which are bad for you, and which should be avoided like the plague. No one can make up your mind for you, so a little research may be in order. It's up to you to make the choice.

Artificial sweeteners are classed as non-nutritive and are also known as *intense sweeteners,* since only a very tiny amount is required to give sweet taste. They provide a sweet sensation to the taste buds without raising blood sugar or insulin levels and may be useful for weight loss or blood sugar/insulin control. Here's what's out there.

Aspartame The most common artificial sweetener is aspartame (sold as Equal and NutraSweet). It's calorie- and carb-free; however, it is far from being an ideal sweetener. It is not chemically stable, meaning that when exposed to heat and air, it breaks down into its chemical constituents: phenylalanine and aspartic acid. That makes it unsuitable for cooking.

Sucralose Sold under the trade name Splenda, sucralose is spun from regular sucrose sugar in such a way that the body doesn't recognize it, so it's not absorbed. Thus it contributes no calories or carbohydrates in its pure form. (Fillers used to give the product bulk do contain carbohydrates; see Fillers on the opposite page.) It remains stable in heat, so it is ideal for cooking and baking. Splenda is available for home use as a bulk sweetener, which measures spoon for spoon exactly the same as sugar.

Acesulfame potassium Many food manufacturers use a combination approach in their products – blending aspartame with another sweetener: acesulfame potassium (also known as acesulfame-K or ace-K). Ace-K tends to have a bitter aftertaste, but that's eliminated when it's combined with another sweetener. By combining sweeteners, an improved sweet taste is achieved and reduced amounts of each chemical are required.

Saccharin Discovered over a century ago, saccharin has been used around the world as a noncalorie sweetener with a relatively high safety record. As a sweetener, saccharin is heat stable but may yield a metallic aftertaste. However, it exerts a synergistic effect when blended with other sweeteners, which minimizes the aftertaste. Saccharin is available as a tabletop sweetener in powder, liquid or tablet form.

Cyclamate This sweetener is available in Canada and Australia, however, though it has EU approval, a granular version is not at present available in the UK. It has not been available in the United States since the 1970s. Cyclamate is stable in heat, so it's fine to use in cooking and baking.

Fillers Artificial sweeteners are very concentrated; only a tiny dot is needed to equal the sweetness of a teaspoon of sugar. Since it's not practical to measure a tiny dot, fillers are necessary to give the products bulk. The most common fillers are maltodextrin, dextrose, lactose and water. Obviously, water has no carbohydrates, so liquid sweeteners contain zero calories, zero carbs. The other ingredients listed are carbohydrates and are digested as sugars. Read the label of your sweetener product carefully so you know what's in it. Fillers will be the source of any calories and carbohydrates listed on the nutrient panel.

Inulin This is a natural soluble fibre extracted from chicory root and has been well-known in Europe for many years for its positive influence on digestive health.

Inulin does have a sweet taste, and because it's a soluble fibre, it can bind with water to give bulk and texture. Thus it has many commercial uses as a fat and sugar replacement. It may also be used in powder form as a filler for artificial sweeteners.

Sugar alcohols In spite of the name, these sweeteners are neither sugars nor alcohols and are sometimes called polyols to avoid confusion. Some sugar alcohols that you may see on ingredient lists include: erythritol, HSH (hydrogenated starch hydrolysate, also called maltitol syrup), isomalt, lactitol, maltitol, mannitol, sorbitol and xylitol.

Sugar alcohols provide the bulk and sweetness of sugar and corn syrup, but they're incompletely absorbed from the intestine. This yields fewer calories and carbs than sugar and results in a much slower and smaller rise in blood glucose and insulin.

Sugar alcohols do yield calories, however – although fewer than sugar, since they're not completely absorbed. Their average calorie content is 2.5 per gram, as opposed to sugar's 4 calories per gram. Be aware that sugar alcohols can cause gastric disturbances and can cause a slow down in fat loss in certain people.

Glycerine This is not a sugar alcohol, although it has similar properties. It's a sweet-tasting syrup. In nature, glycerine molecules are attached to fatty acid molecules to make triglycerides. By itself though, it's not a fat, and it's not technically a sugar or a carbohydrate either. Its most popular dietary use is in sports nutrition because it is quickly absorbed and readily used as fuel by the muscles, without requiring insulin.

The bottom line with sugar alcohols and glycerine is that because of each person's unique chemistry, our bodies can react differently to these chemicals. The sweet taste may trigger emotions that will result in a 'rush' of hormones and enzymes in the body – ultimately leading to an insulin spike and fat storage. Always remember that a sweet is *not* a meal substitute. There's little or no protein, vitamins or essential fatty acids.

HIDE-AND-SEEK: SUGAR IN DISGUISE

It's lurking where you least expect it, and sometimes you need to be a detective to spot sugar in its many forms.

In chemistry, the ending 'ose' indicates sugar; so look out for 'ose' ingredients on food labels. Table sugar – the white granulated type, as well as its brown cousins – is known as sucrose. Other sugars you might encounter include dextrose, fructose, glucose, lactose, and maltose. These sugars are pure carb; thus 1 gram of sugar = 1 gram of carbohydrate = 4 calories.

Check food labels for these other sugar ingredients: barley syrup, corn syrup, demerara sugar, fruit juice concentrate, honey, icing sugar, malt syrup, maple syrup, molasses, rice syrup, Sucanat and turbinado sugar.

Beware of foods that boast 'no added sugar' or 'sugar free' on the label. Many foods such as 'natural' jams and fruit drinks are sweetened with concentrated grape and apple juices, which are very sweet, high-fructose syrups and yield the same carb and calorie counts as table sugar.

Fructose occurs naturally in fruits and vegetables, but it's present in relatively small amounts. In addition, the fibre, pectin, vitamins and minerals in these foods balance the fructose content. On the other hand, fructose that is added to commercially processed food is a highly refined, purified sugar created in a lab from corn syrup, other syrups and chemically treated sucrose sugar.

LIME ANGEL CUSTARD

Makes 8 servings

This custard is like a crème brûlée with a thin, soft, meringue-like top. You can use lemon juice and rind if you prefer or omit both and add 2 teaspoons of pure vanilla extract or another extract.

60 g (2 oz) unsalted butter, at room temperature
12 tbsp Splenda
Grated rind of 3 limes
4 large eggs, separated
2 tbsp finely ground almonds
2 tbsp wheat gluten powder (see page 151)
120 ml (4 fl oz) freshly squeezed lime juice
240 ml (8 fl oz) whipping cream
120 ml (4 fl oz) water

Preheat the oven to 180°C/350°F/gas 4. Place eight 75-ml (5-oz) ramekins in a roasting tin or baking dish.

In a medium bowl, beat the butter, sweetener and lime zest until smooth. Beat in the egg yolks, ground almonds and wheat gluten. Stir in the lime juice, cream and water. It's okay if the mixture looks curdled.

In a clean bowl with clean beaters, beat the egg whites until stiff peaks form. Fold into the lime mixture. Divide among the ramekins. Pour hot water into the larger pan to come halfway up the sides of the ramekins.

Bake for 30–35 minutes, or until puffed and golden brown but still jiggly in the middle. Serve warm, at room temperature, or chilled.

Per serving. Carbohydrates: 4.4 g; Protein: 6.1 g; Fat: 20.6 g; Calories/kJ: 219/917

VANILLA ICE CREAM

Makes 8 servings

This brilliant ice cream was concocted by Wanda – my cooking class assistant and one of the restaurant cooks. A dedicated low-carber, she has a knack for cooking that is rare and wonderful to see.

Note: *If you prefer you can use a whole vanilla bean instead of vanilla extract. Split it lengthwise and heat with the cream. After beating the cream into the egg mixture, retrieve the bean and scrape the tiny black seeds into the custard. Discard the leftover bean or reserve it for another use.*

2 large eggs
5 large egg yolks
720 ml (26 fl oz) whipping cream
16 tbsp Splenda
Large pinch of sea salt
1 tbsp pure vanilla extract

In a large bowl, beat the eggs and egg yolks together with a whisk.

Combine the cream, sweetener and salt in a very large pan. Bring the mixture to a full rolling boil that rises up in the pan (watch it carefully so it doesn't burn).

Immediately start to dribble the cream into the eggs, whisking constantly. After you've added about a third, slowly pour in the remainder, still whisking. Add the vanilla.

Place in the refrigerator and whisk occasionally until cold. Cover and refrigerate until completely chilled, preferably overnight.

Transfer to an ice-cream maker. Churn according to the manufacturer's instructions. Scrape into a storage container and freeze.

Per serving. Carbohydrates: 5 g; Protein: 5.1 g; Fat: 37.5 g; Calories/kJ: 372/1,557

CHOCOLATE SAUCE

Makes 350 ml (12 fl oz)

Totally yummy! And it makes very good hot chocolate syrup. To make hot chocolate, place 2 to 3 tablespoons of the syrup in a mug. Bring a combination of whipping cream and water to the boil and slowly stir into the syrup.

30 g (1 oz) Dutch-processed cocoa powder (see page 150)
300 ml (10 fl oz) water
2 large egg yolks
30 g (1 oz) unsweetened chocolate, finely chopped
60 g (2 oz) unsalted butter, at room temperature
6 tbsp Splenda
Pinch of sea salt
1 tsp pure vanilla extract
1 tsp pure chocolate extract (optional)

Place the cocoa in a small saucepan and slowly whisk in the water to form a smooth paste. Stirring constantly, bring the mixture to the boil over high heat and stir for 1 minute. Remove from the heat.

In a medium bowl, whisk the egg yolks until blended. Whisking constantly, very slowly pour the cocoa mixture into the yolks. Stir in the chocolate, butter, sweetener, salt and extracts and continue stirring until the butter and chocolate have melted. Cool and refrigerate.

Per 1 tbsp. Carbohydrates: 0.7 g; Protein: 0.6 g; Fat: 3 g; Calories/kJ: 31/130

STRAWBERRY SHORTCAKES WITH MASCARPONE BALSAMIC CREAM

Makes 8 servings

The mascarpone cream is out of this world, but you can use sweetened whipped cream with the shortcakes if you like. Feel free to use any berry that's in season.

90 g (3 oz) unsalted butter, at room
    temperature
115 g (4 oz) cream cheese, at room
    temperature
4 large eggs
4 tbsp Splenda
1½ tsp pure vanilla extract
60 ml (2 fl oz) soured cream
145 g (5 oz) finely ground almonds
30 g (1 oz) soya protein isolate powder (see page 151)
30 g (1 oz) wheat gluten powder (see page 151)
1 tsp baking powder
½ tsp bicarbonate of soda
⅛ tsp sea salt

Mascarpone Balsamic Cream (opposite)
500 g (1 lb 2 oz) sliced strawberries

Preheat the oven to 180°C/350°F/gas 4. Line a baking sheet with parchment paper.

In a large bowl, beat the butter and cream cheese until smooth. Beat in the eggs, 1 at a time. Beat in the sweetener, vanilla and soured cream.

In a medium bowl, mix the ground almonds, soya protein, wheat gluten, baking powder, bicarbonate of soda and salt. Add to the cream cheese mixture and beat to mix well.

Place scant 60-ml (2-fl-oz) scoops of the mixture on the prepared baking sheet; you should have 16. With a wet fork, flatten the mounds out into 7.5-cm (2½-in) rounds.

Bake for 10–12 minutes, or until browned.

For each serving, place 1 shortcake on a plate and top with cream and berries. Cover with a second shortcake, more cream and then more berries.

Per serving. Carbohydrates: 10.3 g; Protein: 19.2 g; Fat: 55.2 g; Calories/kJ: 608/2,545

MASCARPONE BALSAMIC CREAM

Makes 8 servings

This is so much more interesting than plain whipped cream. The only trick to making this is to beat the mixture until light and fluffy, but not to the point where it will curdle. This is wonderful on fresh berries and fruit.

340 g (12 oz) mascarpone
4 tbsp Splenda
240 ml (8 fl oz) whipping cream
1 tbsp balsamic vinegar
2 tsp pure vanilla extract

In a medium bowl, beat the mascarpone and sweetener until smooth. Slowly beat in the cream, stopping to scrape down the bowl occasionally, and beat until the mixture turns light and fluffy. Do not overbeat. Stir in the vinegar and vanilla.

Per serving. Carbohydrates: 2.2 g; Protein: 1.6 g; Fat: 10.4 g; Calories/kJ: 104/435

STOCKING UP:
ESSENTIALS FOR LOW-CARB BAKING

Low-carb baking is strange territory to the uninitiated. All these odd potions and powders! Without flour and sugar, the low-carb baker must mimic their action and results. There is no straight-across-the-board substitute for flour, but once you start using low-carb ingredients and gain an understanding of how they work – experimentation is a great teacher – you'll start fitting it all together and using existing low-carb recipes as a springboard for your own wild and wonderful creations.

Almonds, ground Sometimes called almond flour, these are almonds that have been finely ground. They are readily available in supermarkets, but you can also grind your own by pulsing small amounts of the nut in a canister-type coffee grinder. Although you could use a food processor, it's too easy to turn the nuts into almond butter, so you must proceed carefully. Other nuts can also be ground. I think you get the best flavour results by combining them with equal parts ground almonds rather than using them full strength.

Butter, unsalted I've been using unsalted butter for so long that I find salted butter too strong. There are a few reasons why I like to use unsalted butter. First, it's fresher. Salt is a preservative, so you don't know how long salted butter has been hanging around. Salt attracts water, so there is less pure fat and more water in salted butter. And most important, I like to control the salt I'm putting into food.

Chocolate, unsweetened Good-quality chocolate can make all the difference in your desserts. It's deeper and richer in flavour and smoother in texture than regular dark chocolate. Good brands are Valrhona and Menier.

Cocoa powder There are two types of cocoa powder: Dutch-processed and natural unsweetened. Because of their differences, do not substitute one for the other in recipes.

The Dutch version has undergone a technique that alkalizes the cocoa powder to neutralize its acids. Because it is neutral and does not react with baking soda (which needs an acid), it must be used in recipes calling for baking powder – unless there are other acidic ingredients used in sufficient quantities, such as buttermilk or soured cream. It has a reddish-brown colour and mild flavour, and it's easy to dissolve in liquids.

Natural unsweetened cocoa powder tastes bitter and gives a deep chocolate flavour to baked goods. Its intense flavour is suited for use in cookies and some chocolate cakes.

Extracts Good-quality extracts make a huge difference to the flavour of low-carb baked goods and sweets. Buy extracts that are labelled pure.

I can't hide the fact that low-carb desserts and sweets are an expensive endeavour, so why not carry through with the best-tasting extracts?

There's nothing like a pure vanilla extract. Mexican, Madagascar, and Tahitian all have different but equal qualities. You can also get whole vanilla beans, as well as vanilla paste.

Boyajian makes excellent extracts. The fruit ones and citrus oils are brilliant. If you can't buy them locally, try the internet.

Soya protein isolate powder This begins as soya flakes, which are washed to remove most of the carbohydrate content. The protein that's left from the process is then dried, producing an ingredient that is 90 per cent protein based on dry weight. It's much higher in protein than soya flour or soya protein concentrate. Because of its low-carbohydrate content, it's an excellent baking ingredient. You can buy it in good health food shops or through low-carb sites on the internet.

Wheat gluten powder This is the protein of wheat. It makes dough strong and gives it the ability to rise. When you knead bread or beat a batter, you're activating the gluten. Wheat gluten powder cannot be used as a substitute for flour but is great used in conjunction with other ingredients such as soya protein isolate powder, whey protein isolate, ground almonds, fine oatmeal and ground flaxseed (linseed).

The wheat gluten powder you use should be 80 per cent gluten. Though widely available in the US and Canada, elsewhere it is trickier to find so you may need to order it over the internet if it's not available at your local health food shop.

Xanthan gum and guar gum You've probably seen the names on ice cream, yogurt and salad dressing. They're commonly used in the food industry as an emulsifier and stabilizer to thicken gravies, sauces and stir-fries.

Xanthan gum is made by fermenting corn sugar with a microbe. It contains no carbohydrates. A popular low-carb thickener contains a combination of xanthan and guar gums. Unlike guar gum, xanthan gum does not require heat to thicken, and I find the texture to be less waxy than guar gum used alone. You can find it in most good health food shops. These thickeners are best used by combining them with liquids in a blender or with a hand-held blender. In general, ¼ teaspoon is usually enough to thicken 240 ml (8 fl oz) of liquid.

FRESH BERRIES WITH COOL CHAMPAGNE SABAYON

Makes 6 servings

This is a wonderfully festive way of serving fresh berries. Use any combination of summer berries that you like. Sabayon is a French relative of the Italian zabaglione, a warm dessert of whipped egg yolks and Marsala.

Don't let a lack of champagne prevent you from making this. White wine or sparkling wine is quite acceptable as well!

4 large egg yolks
8 tbsp Splenda
120 ml (4 fl oz) dry champagne
240 ml (8 fl oz) whipping cream
320 g (11 oz) raspberries
360 g (12½ oz) strawberries, quartered

In a large heatproof bowl, whisk the egg yolks, sweetener and champagne until smooth. Place over a pan of gently simmering water without letting the bottom of the bowl touch the water. Whisk until thick and increased in volume.

Place the bowl in a larger bowl of ice and let stand until cool, whisking occasionally. Cover and refrigerate.

When you are ready to serve the dessert, whip the cream into soft peaks and fold into the champagne mixture. Divide the berries among 6 wine glasses and top with the sabayon.

Per serving. Carbohydrates: 7.9 g; Protein: 4 g; Fat: 18.5 g; Calories/kJ: 229/959

BASIC ALMOND CRUST

Makes 1 pie crust

This is a perfect crust for cheesecakes or pies. I like to use finely ground almonds because of their neutral flavour. But depending on what you are making, you can replace half of the almonds with another nut. Hazelnut, pecan, walnut and even coconut are all good.

180 g (6½ oz) finely ground almonds
2 tbsp Splenda
¼ tsp sea salt
2 tbsp unsalted butter, melted
1 large egg white

Preheat the oven to 180°C/350°F/gas 4. Line the bottom of a 22.5-cm (9-in) spring-form baking tin or 20-cm (8-in) pie dish with parchment paper. This will prevent the crust from sticking.

In a medium bowl, mix the ground almonds, sweetener and salt. Add the butter and mix well.

In a small bowl, beat the egg white with a whisk until foamy and add to the almond mixture. Stir well and pat into the prepared dish.

Bake for 10–15 minutes, or until a light golden brown. (If the crust rises up, just poke it with a fork and press it down.) Let cool.

Per crust. Carbohydrates: 19.8 g; Protein: 42.8 g; Fat: 117.8 g; Calories/kJ: 1,356/5,676

VARIATIONS
Cinnamon Crust: Add ½ teaspoon cinnamon to the dry ingredients.
Chocolate Crust: Add 2 tablespoons cocoa powder to the dry ingredients.
Crunchy Crust: Replace half of the ground almonds with sliced almonds.

BERRY LEMON PIE

Makes 8 servings

You can use whatever berry – or combination of berries – strikes your fancy.

Lemon Curd (see below), cooled
Basic Almond Crust (page 153), baked and cooled
170 g (6 oz) sliced strawberries
360 ml (12 fl oz) whipping cream
2 tbsp Splenda

Preheat the oven to 180°C/350°F/gas 4.

Spread the lemon curd in the crust and smooth the top. Bake for 30 minutes. Cool completely. Refrigerate for at least 4 hours or overnight.

When ready to serve, spread the strawberries over the top of the pie. Whip the cream and sweetener to firm peaks and pour over the strawberries. Serve immediately.

Per serving. Carbohydrates: 9.8 g; Protein: 9.6 g; Fat: 50.4 g; Calories/kJ: 529/2,214

LEMON CURD

Makes about 480 g (17 oz)

4 large eggs
16 tbsp Splenda
160 ml (5½ fl oz) freshly squeezed lemon juice
Grated rind of 2 lemons
170 g (6 oz) unsalted butter, cut into small pieces

In a large bowl, beat the eggs and sweetener until doubled in volume and light in colour. Gently stir in the lemon juice and rind. Transfer the bowl to the top of a double boiler.

Whisking constantly, cook over simmering water until thickened, about 5 minutes; periodically, use a rubber spatula to scrape the curd from around the sides of the pan. Remove from the heat and stir in the butter until melted. Cool and refrigerate.

Per 480 g (17 oz). Carbohydrates: 40.3 g; Protein: 25.9 g; Fat: 153.2 g; Calories/kJ: 1,592/6,664

RHUBARB COMPOTE

Makes 8 servings

Rhubarb is a nice dessert with a bit of cream. You can spice it up with cinnamon. I like it on the tangy side, so you may want to add more sweetener to this recipe.

455 g (1 lb) fresh young rhubarb with pink stems
2 tbsp water
8 tbsp Splenda

Trim the leaves and the lower end of the stalks from the rhubarb. Cut the stalks into 2.5-cm (1-in) pieces. Place in a non-corrodible saucepan with the water. Cover and set over low heat. Stew gently for 30–45 minutes, until soft. Stir in the sweetener. Cool and refrigerate.

Per serving. Carbohydrates: 3.6 g; Protein: 0.5 g; Fat: 0.1 g; Calories/kJ: 15/63

BE FOOL-ISH!

Fools are old-fashioned desserts made by folding together fruit purée and whipped cream. They have a tangy balance of creamy, sweet and sour. You can make lovely fools with drained Rhubarb Compote or sweetened puréed strawberries, raspberries, blueberries, blackberries or gooseberries.

PUMPKIN TART

Makes 8 generous servings

I grew up with pumpkin tart that my mother made, so for me this is the ultimate.
To toast the nuts, spread them on a baking sheet and bake at 180°C/350°F/gas 4
for 8 minutes.

CRUST

60 ml (2 oz) unsalted butter
100 g (3½ oz) almonds, toasted
100 g (3½ oz) hazelnuts, toasted
6 tbsp whey protein isolate powder (see page 151)
4 tsp Splenda
Pinch of sea salt
¾ tsp ground ginger
½ tsp pure vanilla extract

FILLING

60 ml (2 fl oz) water
2½ tsp gelatine
12 tbsp Splenda
400 g (14 oz) tinned unsweetened pumpkin purée
¾ tsp ground cinnamon
½ tsp ground ginger
½ tsp freshly grated nutmeg
¼ tsp sea salt
1 tsp pure vanilla extract
3 large eggs, separated
480 ml (16 fl oz) whipping cream
¼ tsp cream of tartar

Line the bottom of a 22.5-cm (9-in) pie dish with parchment paper.

To make the crust: Melt the butter in a small saucepan over medium-heat and cook until coloured a deep brown. Remove from the heat.

In a food processor, coarsely grind the almonds and transfer to a large bowl. Coarsely grind the hazelnuts and add to the bowl. Mix in the whey protein, sweetener, salt, ginger and vanilla. Add the butter and mix well. Press evenly into the prepared pie dish. Chill.

To make the filling: Place the water in a small heatproof bowl and sprinkle with the gelatine. Let stand for 2 minutes to soften. Melt the softened gelatine over simmering water or in the microwave.

In a food processor, combine the pumpkin, cinnamon, ginger, nutmeg, salt, vanilla, egg yolks, softened gelatine, 120 ml (4 fl oz) of the cream and 8 tablespoons of the Splenda. Blend until smooth. Transfer to a medium saucepan and cook, stirring constantly, over medium-high heat until the mixture just starts to splutter.

Return the pumpkin mixture to the food processor and blend again until smooth. Transfer to a bowl and let stand at room temperature, stirring frequently, until cool.

In a medium bowl, beat the egg whites until foamy. Add the cream of tartar and the remaining Splenda. Beat until stiff peaks form. Stir one-quarter of the whites into the pumpkin mixture, then fold in the remaining whites. Spread in the prepared crust and refrigerate for at least 2 hours.

Up to 3 hours before serving, beat the remaining whipping cream to firm peaks and pile on top of the pie.

Per serving. Carbohydrates: 10.7 g; Protein: 11.8 g; Fat: 45.3 g; Calories/kJ: 495/2,072

VANILLA PANNA COTTA

Makes 6 servings

This creamy Italian dessert is one of the most adaptable, because the flavours can be changed to suit your fancy or to complement the rest of the meal.

Serve with fresh berries – for a real treat, make them strawberries splashed with balsamic vinegar.

60 ml (2 fl oz) water
2½ tsp gelatine
720 ml (16 fl oz) whipping cream
½ vanilla bean or 2 tsp pure vanilla extract
8 tbsp Splenda

Place the water in a small bowl and sprinkle with the gelatine. Allow it to stand for 2 minutes to soften.

Place half of the cream in a medium saucepan. Slit the vanilla bean lengthwise and add to the pan or add the extract. Bring to the boil, add the gelatine and remove from the heat. Stir until the gelatine dissolves.

Remove the vanilla bean and scrape the seeds into the mixture with the tip of a small knife. Stir in the sweetener and the remaining cream.

Pour into 6 ramekins, dessert dishes or wine glasses. Refrigerate until set, about 4 hours.

If using ramekins, unmould them: dip each ramekin in hot water nearly to its rim for 30 seconds. Run a very thin knife around the inside edge and place a dessert plate over the top. Turn upside down and vigorously shake the ramekin while holding the plate securely. The panna cotta will fall out onto the plate.

Per serving. Carbohydrates: 5.8 g; Protein: 3.3 g; Fat: 44.4 g; Calories/kJ: 423/1,771

TIRAMISU

Makes 8 generous servings

The dessert that makes strong men and women weep! A delicious end to any meal.
Choose a large straight-sided dish, such as a soufflé dish, to assemble the tiramisu.
A straight-sided glass bowl will really show it off!

5 large eggs, separated
8 tbsp Splenda
570 ml (1¼ lb) mascarpone
Basic Almond Sponge Cake (page 161), cooled
120 ml (4 fl oz) strong brewed coffee or espresso
3 tbsp rum
60 g (2 oz) Dutch-processed cocoa (see page 150)

Place the egg yolks and sweetener in a large bowl and beat with an electric mixer until thick and lemon-coloured. Add the mascarpone and beat on low speed, scraping down the bowl as needed, until incorporated. Do not overbeat or the mixture will curdle.

In a clean bowl with clean beaters, beat the egg whites until soft peaks form. Stir one-quarter of the whites into the mascarpone mixture, then fold in the remaining whites.

Cut the cake into 16 fingers (cut it in half crosswise, then lengthwise into 8 slices per half). Combine the coffee and rum in a shallow dish. Place the cocoa in a sieve over a straight-sided serving dish.

Sprinkle the bottom of serving dish with some cocoa. Quickly dip a few of the cake fingers into the coffee mixture and line the bottom of the dish. Do not get them too wet or your tiramisu will be runny. Spread on one-quarter of the mascarpone mixture and dust the top with cocoa.

Repeat the process two or three times so you have three or four layers. End with a sprinkling of cocoa. Cover and refrigerate overnight.

Per serving. Carbohydrates: 5.7 g; Protein: 13.8 g; Fat: 40.8 g; Calories/kJ: 452/1,892

SILKEN CHOCOLATE PUDDING

Makes 8 servings

Soft tofu makes wonderful desserts and is virtually undetectable in the finished product. If you like a lighter chocolate flavour, decrease the chocolate to 60 g (2 oz).

120 ml (4 fl oz) whipping cream
120 ml (4 fl oz) water
Pinch of sea salt
2 large egg yolks
90 g (3 oz) unsweetened chocolate, finely chopped
80 g (2¾ oz) unsalted butter, at room temperature
285 g (10 oz) soft tofu, drained
8 tbsp Splenda
1 tbsp pure chocolate extract (optional)
1 tsp pure vanilla extract

Bring the cream, water and salt to the boil in a small saucepan.

In a small bowl, whisk the egg yolks to blend well. Remove the cream from the heat and slowly whisk a few big spoonfuls into the yolks to warm them. Then whisk in the remaining cream. Pour into the saucepan.

Place over low heat and stir constantly with a heatproof rubber spatula until the cream thickens. Immediately add the chocolate and butter. Remove from the heat and stir constantly until the chocolate and butter are melted. It will look curdled and that's fine.

In a food processor, combine the tofu, sweetener and extracts; blend until smooth. Add the chocolate mixture and blend again until well-combined. Transfer to a bowl and chill for at least 4 hours.

Per serving. Carbohydrates: 4.5 g; Protein: 4.6 g; Fat: 21.5 g; Calories/kJ: 220/921

BASIC ALMOND SPONGE CAKE

Makes 1 cake

This sponge can be the base for all kinds of delectable treats. Layer it with whipped cream and strawberries or with Lemon Curd (page 154) and frost with whipped cream.

115 g (4 oz) finely ground almonds
1 tsp baking powder
¼ tsp sea salt
6 large eggs, at room temperature
8 tbsp Splenda
1 tsp pure vanilla extract

Preheat the oven to 180°C/350°F/gas 4. Butter a 37.5- × 25-cm (15- × 10-in) Swiss roll tin. Line with parchment paper and butter again.

In a small bowl, mix the ground almonds, baking powder and salt.

Place the eggs and sweetener in a large bowl. With an electric mixer, beat until thick, light and tripled in volume, 8–10 minutes. Beat in the vanilla. Fold in the almond mixture. Spread evenly in the prepared tin.

Bake for 20–25 minutes, until the top springs back when pressed lightly. Cool in the tin on a wire rack.

Per cake. Carbohydrates: 27.2 g; Protein: 62.6 g; Fat: 93.4 g; Calories/kJ: 1,176/4,923

CREAM CHEESE, COCONUT AND LEMON MOUNDS

Makes 20 mounds

If you use coconut milk instead of the whipping cream, these little coconutty bites will be even more coconutty. Keep the mounds refrigerated or frozen to prevent spoilage – assuming they would last that long!

90 g (3 oz) unsweetened desiccated coconut
2 tbsp Splenda
120 ml (4 fl oz) whipping cream
½ tsp pure vanilla extract
60 g (2 oz) cream cheese, at room temperature
1 large egg
½ tsp finely grated lemon rind

In a medium bowl, mix the coconut, sweetener, cream and vanilla. Let stand for 1 hour.

Preheat the oven to 180°C/350°F/gas 4. Line a baking sheet with parchment paper.

Stir the cream cheese into the coconut mixture until blended. Add the egg and mix well. Stir in the lemon rind.

Drop by level tablespoons (making macaroon-shaped mounds), 5 cm (2 in) apart, on the prepared baking sheet. Bake for about 15 minutes, until the tops are lightly speckled with brown.

Per mound. Carbohydrates: 0.7 g; Protein: 0.8 g; Fat: 5.4 g; Calories/kJ: 54/226

NUT BUTTER–FROSTED BROWNIES

Makes 24 brownies

These cake-type brownies get rave reviews. You can use almond or hazelnut butter as an alternative to peanut butter. Roasted almond butter is my favourite for a sophisticated chocolate icing.

Tamarian – the founder and Webmaster of lowcarber.org – came up with this wonderful recipe.

BROWNIES

3 large eggs
115 g (4 oz) unsalted butter, melted
60 ml (2 fl oz) water
3 tbsp soured cream
8 tbsp Splenda
1 tsp pure vanilla extract
45 g (1½ oz) finely ground almonds
75 g (2½ oz) fine oatmeal
30 g (1 oz) Dutch-processed cocoa powder (see page 150)
1½ tsp baking powder

FROSTING

30 g (1 oz) unsweetened chocolate
1 tbsp natural peanut butter
40 ml (2 fl oz) whipping cream
4 tbsp Splenda

Preheat the oven to 180°C/350°F/gas 4. Butter a 22.5- × 22.5-cm (9- × 9-in) baking tin.

To make the brownies: In a large bowl, beat the eggs for a few minutes until light and fluffy. Add the butter, water, soured cream, sweetener and vanilla. Beat the mixture until combined.

In a small bowl, mix the ground almonds, oatmeal, cocoa and baking powder. Add to the egg mixture and beat until well-blended. Pour the batter into the prepared baking tin.

Bake for 25 minutes, until the top is firm. Let cool on a wire rack.

To make the frosting: Melt the chocolate in a heatproof bowl over simmering water or in the microwave. Stir in the peanut butter until melted, then stir in the cream and sweetener. Pour over the cooled brownies and spread evenly. Let the frosting set before cutting.

Per brownie. Carbohydrates: 2.8 g; Protein: 2.3 g; Fat: 8.3 g; Calories/kJ: 93/389

CHOCOLATE: QUALITY RULES!

I can't stress this enough: use high-quality chocolate. The graininess of cheap brands really becomes apparent when they're used in low-carb cooking. And they just can't compare in depth of flavour with first-rate chocolate.

COURGETTE CAKE

Makes 12 servings

Oh joy! This tastes exactly like a carrot cake! It's a big cake that's moist and rich. Bring it to the table to cut it so everyone can ooh and aah over how good it looks.

285 g (10 oz) cream cheese, at room temperature
170 g (6 oz) unsalted butter, at room temperature
20 tbsp Splenda
7 large eggs
455 g (1 lb) courgettes (zucchini), grated and squeezed dry
1 tbsp pure vanilla extract
285 g (10 oz) finely ground almonds
60 g (2 oz) finely chopped walnuts
60 g (2 oz) unsweetened desiccated coconut
5 tbsp ground cinnamon
1 tbsp Dutch-processed cocoa powder (see page 150)
1½ tsp baking powder
½ tsp sea salt
Orange Cream Cheese Frosting (page 168)

Preheat the oven to 180°C/350°F/gas 4. Butter two 20-cm (8-in) cake tins and line the bottoms with parchment paper.

In a large bowl, beat the cream cheese and butter until smooth. Add the sweetener and beat until combined. Beat in the eggs, one at a time, blending well after each addition. Stir in the courgette (zucchini) and vanilla.

In a medium bowl, mix the ground almonds, walnuts, coconut, cinnamon, cocoa, baking powder and salt. Stir into the courgette (zucchini) mixture. Divide the batter evenly between the prepared tins.

Bake for 35 minutes, or until the layers are firm to the touch. Cool on a wire rack for 5 minutes. Turn the layers out onto the rack to cool completely.

(continued on page 168)

Place 1 layer on a cake stand or serving platter. Spread the top with frosting. Top with the second layer and frost the top and sides. Refrigerate until the frosting is set. Store, covered, in the refrigerator.

Per serving. Carbohydrates: 11.5 g; Protein: 16.9 g; Fat: 71.5 g; Calories/kJ: 748/3,131

ORANGE CREAM CHEESE FROSTING

Makes about 720 ml (1½ pints)

Instead of orange rind as a flavouring, you could use lemon rind, freshly grated ginger or maple extract to complement whatever cake you're using it on.

500 g (18 oz) cream cheese, at room temperature
230 g (8 oz) unsalted butter, at room temperature
12 tbsp Splenda
1 tbsp pure vanilla extract
2 tsp finely grated orange rind

In a medium bowl, beat the cream cheese and butter until smooth. Beat in the sweetener, vanilla and orange rind. Continue beating until fluffy.

Per 60 ml (2 fl oz). Carbohydrates: 3.2 g; Protein: 3.2 g; Fat: 30.1 g; Calories/kJ: 289/1,210

INDEX

Underscored page references indicate boxed text. **Boldfaced** page references indicate photographs.

OTHER RODALE BOOKS
AVAILABLE FROM PAN MACMILLAN

1-4050-7749-2	The Greek Doctor's Diet	*Dr Fedon Alexander Lindberg*	£9.99
1-4050-6717-9	The South Beach Diet Cookbook	*Dr Arthur Agatston*	£20
1-4050-8775-7	The South Beach Diet Good Fats/Good Carbs Guide	*Dr Arthur Agatston*	£4.99
1-4050-7771-9	The Great American Detox Diet	*Alex Jamieson*	£10.99
1-4050-0665-X	Get a Real Food Life	*Janine Whiteson*	£12.99
1-4050-7753-0	The Thin Commandments	*Dr Stephen Gullo*	£10.99

All Rodale/Pan Macmillan titles can be ordered from the website, *www.panmacmillan.com*, or from your local bookshop and are also available by post from:

Bookpost, PO Box 29, Douglas, Isle of Man IM99 1BQ
Tel: 01624 677237; fax: 01624 670923; e-mail: *bookshop@enterprise.net*; or
visit: *www.bookpost.co.uk*. Credit cards accepted. Free postage and packing in the
United Kingdom

Prices shown above were correct at time of going to press.
Pan Macmillan reserve the right to show new retail prices on covers which may differ from
those previously advertised in the text or elsewhere.

For information about buying *Rodale* titles in **Australia**, contact Pan Macmillan Australia.
Tel: 1300 135 113; fax: 1300 135 103;
e-mail: *customer.service@macmillan.com.au*; or visit: *www.panmacmillan.com.au*

For information about buying *Rodale* titles in **New Zealand**, contact Macmillan Publishers
New Zealand Limited. Tel: (09) 414 0356; fax: (09) 414 0352;
e-mail: *lyn@macmillan.co.nz*; or visit: *www.macmillan.co.nz*

For information about buying *Rodale* titles in **South Africa**, contact Pan Macmillan South
Africa. Tel: (011) 325 5220; fax: (011) 325 5225;
e-mail: *marketing@panmacmillan.co.za*

RODALE

MACMILLAN